# Contents

Printed in the U.S.A

ISBN 13: 978-0-618-54060-0

11 12 -1413- 16 15 14 13 12 11 10

4500251384

# UNIT 1 Land and First People

## CHAPTER 1 The Geography of California

## CHAPTER 2 The First Californians

# UNIT 2 Exploration and Colonization

## CHAPTER 3 Spanish California

## CHAPTER 4 Mexican California

# UNIT 3 New Flags for California

## CHAPTER 5 The Gold Rush Years

# UNIT 4  California Changes

## CHAPTER 12 The Twenty-first Century

*Practice Book*

viii

# Almanac Map Practice

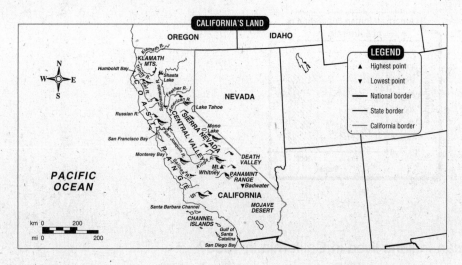

Use the map to do these activities and answer these questions.

## Practice

1. Draw a circle around the highest point in California. Draw a square
   around the lowest point in California.

   _____

   _____

2. Look to the north of California. Which state shares California's

   northern border? _____

3. About how many miles is it from San Francisco Bay to Lake Tahoe?

   _____

4. What is west of California? _____

5. What river flows into Monterey Bay? _____

## Apply

6. With a partner, look at the map above. Find the region of California
   where you live and draw a circle around it. Look on the map for a
   natural feature nearest to your home. It can be a river, a lake, the
   ocean, or a mountain. Draw a triangle around the feature's name.
   Then write that name on the line below.

   _____

   _____

**1**                **Use with *California Studies*, pp. 2–3**

# Almanac Graph Practice

**American Indian Population of California**

## Practice

**1.** How many American Indians lived in California in 1500?

_____

**2.** How many American Indians lived in California in 2000?

_____

**3.** What is the difference between the number of American Indians who lived in California in 1500 and the number who lived in 2000?

_____

## Apply

Read the paragraph below. Then use the information in it to complete the chart below.

> American Indians live in all 50 states of the United States. For example, 10,725 American Indians live in Rhode Island. Oklahoma has the second largest number of American Indians after California, with 391,949. Delaware has the fewest American Indians with 6,069.

| STATE | AMERICAN INDIANS |
|---|---|
| **4.** _____ | _____ |
| **5.** _____ | _____ |
| **6.** _____ | _____ |

*Practice Book*
2
Use with *California Studies*, p. 3

# Vocabulary and Study Guide

## Vocabulary

Write the definition of each vocabulary word below.

| geography | continent | equator | hemisphere |

**1.** geography _____

_____

**2.** continent _____

_____

**3.** equator _____

_____

**4.** hemisphere _____

## Study Guide

**5.** Read "California's Location." Then fill in the blanks below.

There are many ways to describe California's location. First, it is

in the Northern _____. This means that California lies

north of the _____. Second, it is on the

_____ of North America. California also lies between

_____ in the north and Mexico in the south.

**6.** Read "Geographers Ask Four Questions." Then fill in the web below.

a.

b.

**Questions geographers ask**

c.

d.

# Skillbuilder: Review Map Skills

## Practice

**1.** What is the symbol for city? What city is north of Sacramento?

_____

**2.** How many miles would you have to travel to go from San Francisco to Sacramento?

_____

**3.** What is the symbol for a volcanic peak? List two volcanic peaks in California.

_____

## Apply

**4.** Use your map skills to find the mystery city on the map. The mystery city is north of Fresno, west of Sacramento, and south of San Francisco. What is the city? How did you find the city?

_____

_____

_____

# Vocabulary and Study Guide

## Vocabulary

If you do not know a long word's meaning, try breaking it into smaller parts. It may contain smaller words that you know.

| New Word | Words in it that I know | Word meanings that I know | What I think the word means |
|---|---|---|---|
| **1.** landform | | | |

Use each of the following words in a sentence.

**2.** delta _____

_____

**3.** environment _____

_____

## Study Guide

Read "Land and Water." Then choose the correct ending to each statement.

**4.** Volcanoes and earthquakes changed California's ____

    **a.** people.             **b.** ranges.             **c.** landforms.

**5.** Many valleys and canyons were formed due to ____

    **a.** earthquakes.        **b.** erosion.             **c.** landforms.

Read "California's Water." Then choose the correct ending to each statement.

**6.** In the Sierra Nevada there are two lakes created partly by ____

    **a.** glaciers.           **b.** volcanoes.        **c.** people.

**7.** Conservation means protecting ____

    **a.** the environment.    **b.** roads.           **c.** people.

# Vocabulary and Study Guide

## Vocabulary

Draw a line connecting the vocabulary word to its meaning.

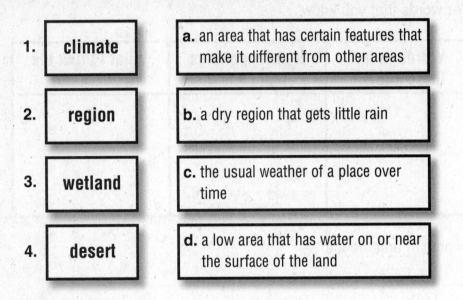

1. **climate**

   **a.** an area that has certain features that make it different from other areas

2. **region**

   **b.** a dry region that gets little rain

3. **wetland**

   **c.** the usual weather of a place over time

4. **desert**

   **d.** a low area that has water on or near the surface of the land

## Study Guide

5. Read "Climate." Then fill in the blanks below.

> Three things affect climate. First, places that are closer to the _____ are usually warmer than places that are farther away. Second, the place that is closer to a large body of _____ is warmer than places inland. Last, the higher a place is in elevation, the _____ its climate is.

6. Read "Regions of California." Then fill in the Main Idea and Details chart.

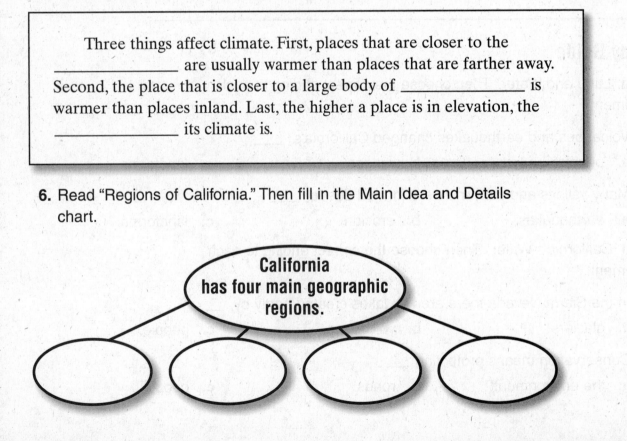

California has four main geographic regions.

# Skillbuilder: Use Latitude and Longitude

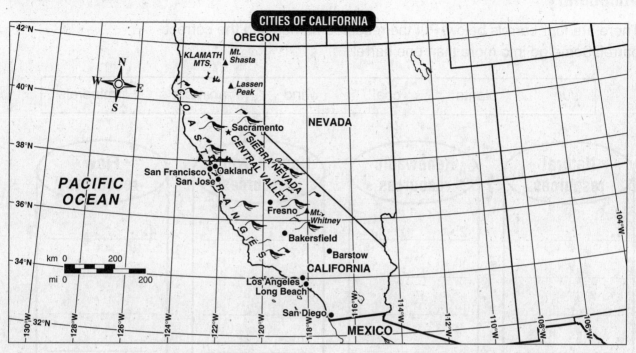

Use the map to answer these questions.

## Practice

1. Which city is north of 38°N latitude? _____

2. Which cities are at about 117°W longitude? _____

3. What is the latitude of California's northern border? _____

4. What is the longitude of San Jose? _____

## Apply

5. Name a city that is close to 34°N latitude, 118°W longitude.

_____

_____

6. Which city is closest to 35°N longitude, 119°W latitude?

_____

# Vocabulary and Study Guide

## Vocabulary

There are four barrels below. Put the resource named into the correct barrel. Some go into more than one barrel.

| sun | plants | coal | wind | animals | minerals |

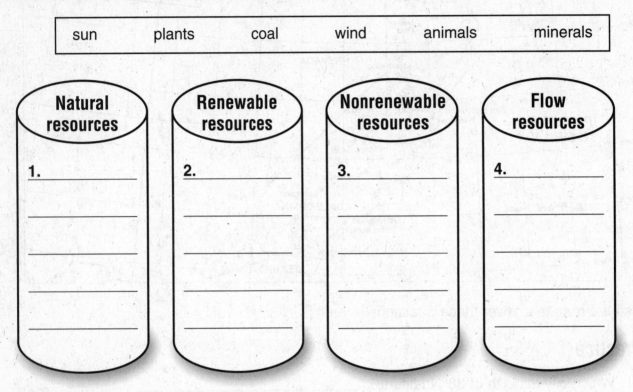

**Natural resources**

1. _____

_____

_____

_____

_____

**Renewable resources**

2. _____

_____

_____

_____

_____

**Nonrenewable resources**

3. _____

_____

_____

_____

_____

**Flow resources**

4. _____

_____

_____

_____

_____

## Study Guide

Read "Using Resources." Then fill in the causes and effects in the chart below.

**Causes**          **Effects**

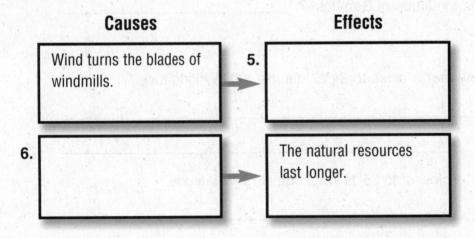

Wind turns the blades of windmills.

5. _____

6. _____

The natural resources last longer.

**Use with** *California Studies*, pp. 30–33

# Vocabulary and Study Guide

## Vocabulary

Read each definition below. Then write the word from the box that goes with it in the blank.

| | | |
|---|---|---|
| adapt | diversity | oral history |

1. _____ variety

2. _____ an account of events told through speaking

3. _____ change in order to live in a new environment

## Study Guide

Read "California's First People" and "Different Communities." Then fill in the chart below to compare California during and after the last Ice Age.

| During the Ice Age | After the Ice Age |
|---|---|
| 4. | 5. |

6. Read "Different Communities." Then fill in the blanks below.

California has many different types of environments. Each Indian group had to adjust or _____ to the resources where it lived. Over time, the way of life of California's Indian groups became very different. The amount of _____ or variety among the groups grew. There were many _____, or groups of people living in the same place under the same laws. These were made up of 500 Indian _____, each with its own chief.

# Vocabulary and Study Guide

## Vocabulary

Read the clues and write the answers in the blanks. Then find the word in the puzzle. Look up, down, forward, and backward.

1. the exchange of resources, goods, or services

   _____

2. trade without the use of money _____

3. something that can be bought and sold _____

4. the way in which a group uses its resources to make,

   buy, and sell things _____

5. work people do for others _____

| S | L | M | N | Z | X | W |
|---|---|---|---|---|---|---|
| E | C | O | N | O | M | Y |
| R | E | T | R | A | B | C |
| V | T | R | A | D | E | M |
| I | U | O | K | B | Y | R |
| C | F | L | G | O | O | D |
| E | V | S | T | W | A | B |

## Study Guide

Read "Living on the Coast." Then read each description in the boxes on the left below. In each box on the right, write the name of the California Indian group described. You may use each group more than once.

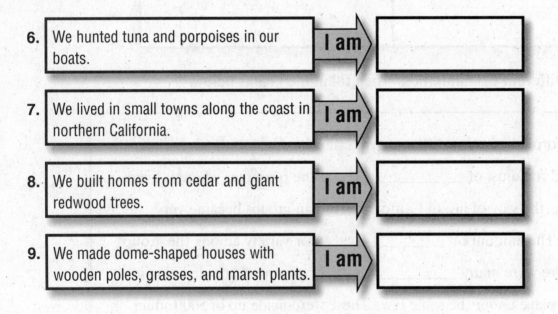

6. We hunted tuna and porpoises in our boats. **I am**

7. We lived in small towns along the coast in northern California. **I am**

8. We built homes from cedar and giant redwood trees. **I am**

9. We made dome-shaped houses with wooden poles, grasses, and marsh plants. **I am**

*Practice Book*
**10**
Use with *California Studies*, pp. 48–51

# Skillbuilder: Use Reference Materials

| Reference Material | How to Find Information |
|---|---|
| An atlas contains many different kinds of maps. ATLAS OF THE WORLD | Look in the index for the location you want to find. The index is in the back of the atlas. It is an alphabetized list of locations included in the book. |
| An encyclopedia has information about people, places, and events. | Find the volume that includes the first letter of the topic. If your topic isn't listed, think of a bigger idea that your topic might be a part of. |
| An Internet website is a source of information that can be found online by using a computer. | Type your topic into a search engine. A search engine is a website that helps you find other websites. A search engine will show you a list of websites related to the topic. |

## Practice

1. Steatite, a soft stone from the islands, was a prized resource. Which encyclopedia volume would you use to find out more about it?

_____

2. What key words could you type into an Internet search engine to find out about things the Chumash used?

_____

## Apply

Write one question about a group of California Indians you read about in the chapter. Use one or more of the reference materials listed above to answer the question. Write down which source materials you used.

3. _____

_____

_____

_____

**11**

# Vocabulary and Study Guide

## Vocabulary

Use each of the following vocabulary words in a sentence. The sentences should summarize the lesson.

1. culture _____

_____

2. tradition _____

_____

3. ceremony _____

_____

## Study Guide

Read "Valley and Mountain Life." Then choose the correct ending to each sentence.

4. People of the mountains built sturdy cone-shaped houses made of

_____.

   **a.** tree bark        **b.** grasses        **c.** bricks

5. The Yokuts of the Central Valley made light shelters out of

_____.

   **a.** wood        **b.** adobe        **c.** grasses

6. The Miwoks and Yokuts of the Sierra Nevada hunted

_____.

   **a.** deer and bears        **b.** bison and elk        **c.** rabbits and snakes

7. Read "California Indian Religions." Then complete the sequence chart.

| California Indians began certain traditions in their culture. | → | | → | Today, California Indians still know about and practice traditions from their culture. |
|---|---|---|---|---|

# Vocabulary and Study Guide

## Vocabulary

Write the definition of each vocabulary word below.

**1.** hunter-gatherer _____

_____

**2.** agriculture _____

**3.** government _____

_____

**4.** leadership _____

## Study Guide

**5.** Read "Adapting to the Desert." Then fill in the blanks below.

California Indians of the desert used its _____ to

get the foods they needed. They gathered more than 100 types of

nuts, roots, seeds, and _____. California Indians took

_____ from the desert's streams. They ground up the

_____ of mesquite trees to make mush or cakes.

**6.** Read "Government." Then fill in the blanks below.

Most California Indians saw themselves as part of a group. They

organized themselves in _____ that shared an

ancestor. Small groups of desert people usually had their own

separate _____. The _____

were different. All the members of this nation saw themselves as

one large group. During _____, their towns all

fought together against enemies.

**13**     **Use with *California Studies*, pp. 64–67**

# Almanac Map Practice

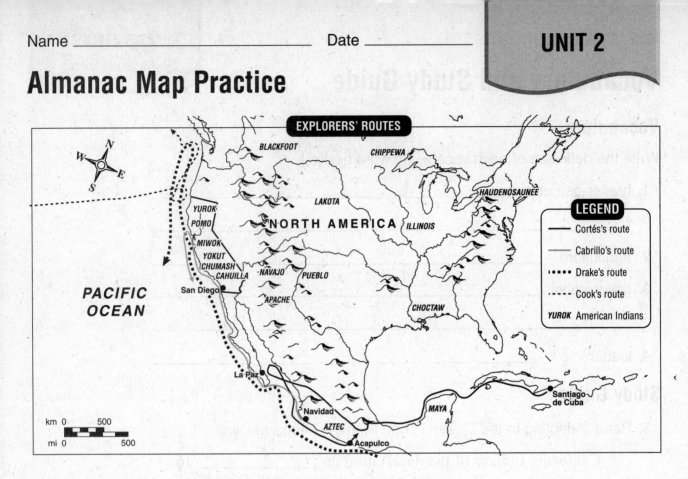

Use the map to do these activities and answer these questions.

## Practice

1. Draw a line along Juan Cabrillo's route.

2. Which part of North America did James Cook explore?

   _____

   _____

3. Circle the area explored by Hernán Cortés.

4. How many explorers' routes are shown? _____

## Apply

With a partner, look at a current map of North America in your textbook.
Find the areas explored by Juan Cabrillo, Francis Drake, and Hernán
Cortés. Write the names of the areas.

   _____

   _____

# Almanac Graph Practice

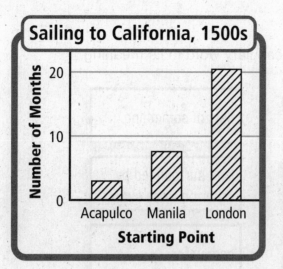

**Sailing to California, 1500s**

Number of Months / Starting Point
Acapulco   Manila   London

## Practice

**1.** Which route had the shortest travel time by ship?

_____

**2.** How long did it take to sail from Manila to California in the 1500s?

_____

## Apply

**3.** Use the information below to complete the bar graph.

### Early Airplanes

| Airplane | Speed (in mph) |
|---|---|
| Vega | 150 |
| Boeing Stratoliner | 200 |
| DC-7 | 300 |

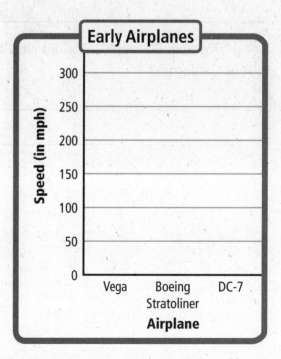

**Early Airplanes**

Speed (in mph) / Airplane
Vega   Boeing Stratoliner   DC-7

*Practice Book*
**15**   **Use with *California Studies*, p. 77**

# Vocabulary and Study Guide

## Vocabulary

**1.** Draw a line connecting the vocabulary word to its meaning.

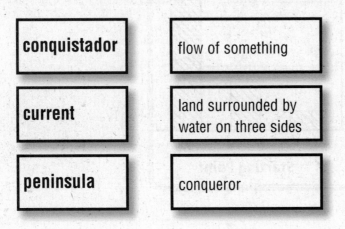

| | |
|---|---|
| **conquistador** | flow of something |
| **current** | land surrounded by water on three sides |
| **peninsula** | conqueror |

## Study Guide

**2.** Read "A Search for Riches." What are some reasons explorers came to North America?

_____

_____

**3.** Read "Exploring the Coast." Why was Spain more interested in Asia than in California?

_____

**4.** Read "Physical Barriers." Why did New Spain stop sending explorers to Alta California?

_____

_____

**16**  **Use with *California Studies*, pp. 80–85**

# Skillbuilder: Make a Map

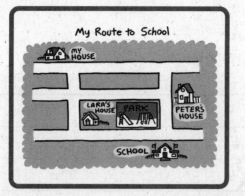

## Practice

1. Whose house is closest to the park? _____

2. Draw a route on the map that starts at school, passes Lara's house, passes Peter's house, and ends at the park. In the box next to the map, make a legend for your route line.

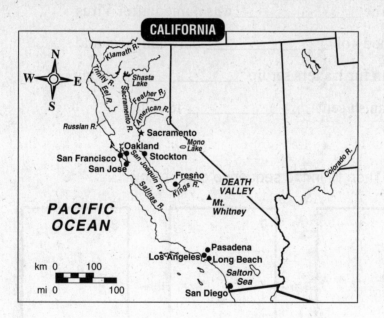

## Apply

Follow these directions to mark a route on the California map.

1. Start in San Francisco and go south to San Jose.

2. From San Jose, go south to Pasadena.

3. Take a bus north to Sacramento.

4. Go north to Shasta Lake.

**17**        Use with *California Studies*, pp. 88–89

# Vocabulary and Study Guide

## Vocabulary

Write the definition of the vocabulary word below.

**1.** colony _____

**2.** settler _____

**3.** missionary _____

**4.** mission _____

_____

## Study Guide

**5.** Read "Seeking New Routes." Then fill in the blanks below.

Europeans in the 1700s looked for routes from North America

to _____. The _____ was named after Vitus

Bering. It is a narrow body of _____ between Asia and

North America. Russian fur traders set up _____ along

Alaska's coast. The Spanish sent _____ to Alta

California in 1768.

Read "A Major Expedition." Then fill in the sequence chart below.

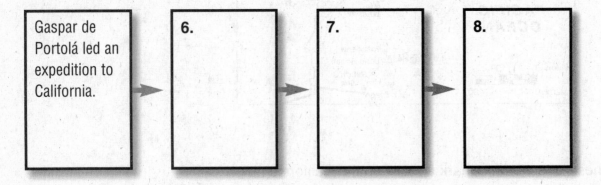

Gaspar de Portolá led an expedition to California. → **6.** → **7.** → **8.**

**Use with** *California Studies,* **pp. 90–93**

# Skillbuilder: Make a Timeline

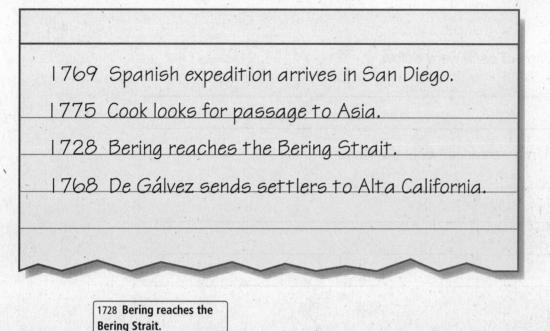

1769  Spanish expedition arrives in San Diego.

1775  Cook looks for passage to Asia.

1728  Bering reaches the Bering Strait.

1768  De Gálvez sends settlers to Alta California.

1728 **Bering reaches the Bering Strait.**

1720                                                1780

## Practice

1. Label the years between 1720 and 1780 on the timeline.

2. How many years are covered in the timeline? _____

3. Look at the events listed in the box. Write the events into the timeline. One is already done for you.

## Apply

4. Who explored first, Vitus Bering or Captain James Cook? _____

5. Did José de Gálvez send settlers to California before or after the Spanish arrived at San Diego? _____

6. What happened seven years after 1768? _____

_____

**19**    Use with *California Studies*, pp. 96–97

# Vocabulary and Study Guide

## Vocabulary

Write the definition of each word below.

**1.** convert _____

**2.** revolt _____

Use each word in a sentence about the lesson.

**3.** _____

_____

**4.** _____

_____

## Study Guide

**5.** Read "Life at a Mission." Then fill in the blanks below.

Some California Indians gave up their way of life and

became _____. They stayed with the priests on the

_____. Many of them worked in the fields on mission

_____. They learned to raise farm _____.

Using both kindness and cruel treatment, the priests made many

Indians _____ from their old beliefs.

**6.** Read "Life at a Mission." Then fill in the cause and effect chart below.

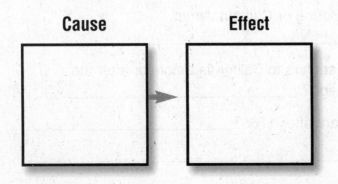

**Cause**          **Effect**

# Vocabulary and Study Guide

## Vocabulary

**Across**

2. The leader of a pueblo
3. A fort

**Down**

1. A person who leads a colony or state
3. A town or village

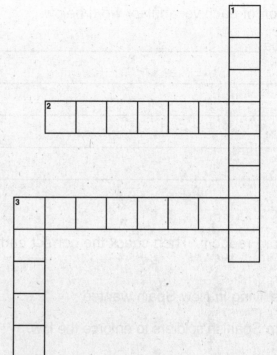

## Study Guide

Read "Starting Pueblos." Then fill in the cause and effect chart below.

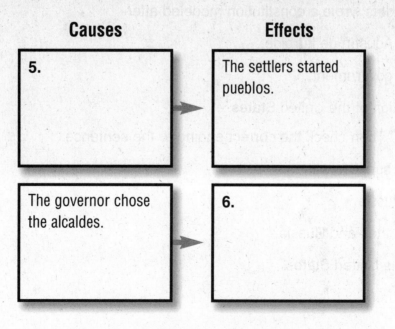

| Causes | Effects |
|--------|---------|
| 5. | The settlers started pueblos. |
| The governor chose the alcaldes. | 6. |

# Vocabulary and Study Guide

## Vocabulary

Write the definition of each vocabulary word below.

1. independence _____

2. constitution _____

3. republic _____

4. import _____

5. export _____

## Study Guide

Read "Fighting for Freedom." Then check the correct ending to the sentence below.

6. Many people living in New Spain wanted

_____ a. more Spanish soldiers to enforce the law.

_____ b. greater rights and freedoms.

_____ c. to work hard for the viceroy.

Read "The Republic of Mexico." Then check the correct ending to the sentence below.

7. In 1824, Mexico's leaders wrote a constitution modeled after

_____ a. the ideas of Agustín de Iturbide.

_____ b. the Spanish government.

_____ c. the Constitution of the United States.

Read "Trade in California." Then check the correct ending to the sentence.

8. Californios traded for supplies with

_____ a. Spain and Russia.

_____ b. the United States and Russia.

_____ c. Spain and the United States.

# Vocabulary and Study Guide

## Vocabulary

Read the clue and write the answer in the blank. Then find the word in the puzzle. Look up, down, forward, and backward.

1. Land that is given away

   is called a _____.

2. An assembly, or group, of citizens that helps

   make laws is called a _____.

3. _____ is when the government takes over property that belongs to a church.

4. A _____ is another name for a cattle ranch.

| A | R | B | H | I | N | G | O | X |
|---|---|---|---|---|---|---|---|---|
| D | W | M | Q | C | O | Z | E | L |
| Y | D | T | D | E | I | O | R | B |
| P | I | Y | U | V | T | X | S | K |
| L | P | I | G | N | A | R | D | H |
| E | U | W | Q | G | Z | J | C | D |
| Y | T | I | B | H | I | E | S | S |
| L | A | N | D | G | R | A | N | T |
| Y | C | R | D | B | A | V | E | M |
| N | I | J | K | R | L | D | E | W |
| T | O | U | F | S | U | X | O | P |
| Z | N | G | O | H | C | N | A | R |
| H | E | T | W | V | E | U | F | Y |
| F | V | L | S | B | S | R | T | K |

## Study Guide

5. Read "Change in Alta California." Then fill in the blanks below.

   Californios were cut off from the rest of _____ by mountains and deserts. But when the fight for freedom ended, they accepted the new government of _____. All California Indians and Californios were considered _____ of Mexico. A _____ was set up in Monterey to make laws for the Californios, but it had little power.

6. Read "The End of the Missions." Then fill in the blanks below.

   After Mexico won independence, the new government _____ most of the land that had belonged to the Catholic Church. _____ were given to rich Californios and new settlers. Many land grants became large _____. These cattle ranches helped California's _____.

# Vocabulary and Study Guide

## Vocabulary

Read the definitions below. Then write the word that goes with it in the blank.

1. A man who owns a rancho _____

2. A cowboy _____

3. A party or celebration _____

4. Spanish word for roundup _____

5. A woman who owns a rancho _____

## Study Guide

Read "The Rise of the Ranchos." Then fill in the sequence chart below.

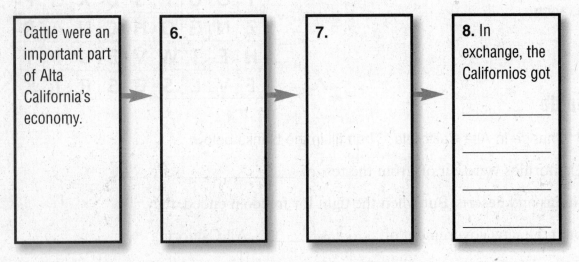

| Cattle were an important part of Alta California's economy. | **6.** | **7.** | **8.** In exchange, the Californios got _____ _____ _____ _____ |

9. Read "Living in a Pueblo." Then fill in the blanks below.

Pueblos began as small _____ towns. They were

used by _____ and _____ to store hides and

tallow. Traders came by _____ to pueblos near the coast.

The landing of a ship was usually an excuse for a party called a

_____, which often lasted several days. California

Indians who had no land often worked for food and shelter as

_____ on _____.

# Vocabulary and Study Guide

## Vocabulary

Write the definition of each vocabulary word below.

**1.** pioneer _____

**2.** trapper _____

**3.** frontier _____

Use each word in a sentence about the lesson.

**4.** _____

_____

**5.** _____

**6.** _____

## Study Guide

**7.** Read "Explorers Cross the Frontier." Then fill in the blanks below.

    Word got back to the United States of the warm climate and

natural resources of _____. Mountain men began to

cross the _____ to visit Alta California. A mountain

man named Jedediah Strong Smith was the first to cross the

dangerous _____ to get there. John C. Frémont

explored mountain passes and made _____ of them.

_____ found the safest pass through the mountains,

and it was named after him.

Read "Pioneers Move West." Then complete the chart.

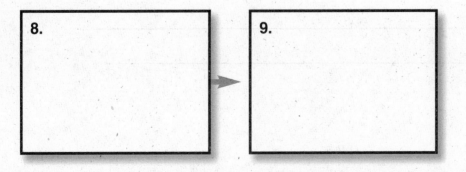

**8.**

**9.**

**Use with *California Studies*, pp. 138–143**

# Skillbuilder: Write a Report

California's climate drew settlers across the frontier.

## Practice

**1.** Where could you go to find information about this topic?

_____

**2.** What might be some keywords and phrases you could use to do an Internet search about this topic?

_____

**3.** When you take notes about the main topic, what two things should you do?

_____

**4.** How could you organize your notes to write this report?

_____

## Apply

Read "Sutter's Fort" in Lesson 4. Then use the steps you learned for writing a report to write the introductory paragraph of a report about John Augustus Sutter.

_____

_____

_____

_____

**Use with *California Studies*, pp. 148–149**

# Almanac Map Practice

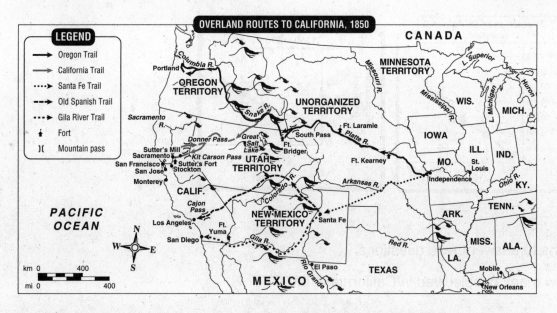

**OVERLAND ROUTES TO CALIFORNIA, 1850**

**LEGEND**
→ Oregon Trail
⟹ California Trail
••••► Santa Fe Trail
– –► Old Spanish Trail
-•-•► Gila River Trail
⚑ Fort
)( Mountain pass

Use the map to do these activities and answer these questions.

## Practice

**1.** Which trails could settlers follow from Independence, Missouri, to California's Gold Rush region?

_____

_____

**2.** Find the mountain passes that led across the mountains in eastern California to the Gold Rush region. Which one was farther north?

_____

_____

**3.** Which city is at the western end of the California Trail? _____

**4.** Which trails did settlers follow from Independence, Missouri, to Los Angeles? _____

**5.** About how long was the California Trail? _____

## Apply

With a partner, find the Sacramento River on the map above. Follow its route to San Francisco, where it empties into the bay. Then, on a separate sheet of paper, explain how the Sacramento River could have been important to miners.

*Practice Book*
**27**                          Use with *California Studies*, p. 156

# Almanac Graph Practice

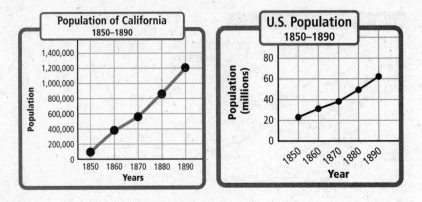

## Practice

Use the graphs to answer these questions.

**1.** About how many people lived in California in 1850?

_____

**2.** Which was greater, the California population in 1890 or the U.S.

population in 1850?

_____

## Apply

**3.** Use the information below to complete the bar graph.

### U.S. Population, 1980–2000

| Year | Population |
|------|------------|
| 1980 | 227,726,000 |
| 1990 | 250,132,000 |
| 2000 | 282,434,000 |

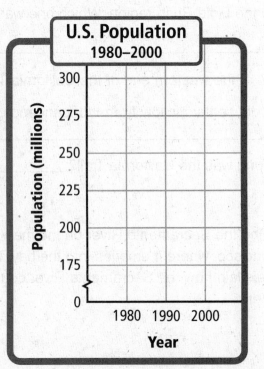

# Vocabulary and Study Guide

## Vocabulary

Write the definition of each vocabulary word below.

**1.** official _____

**2.** headquarters _____

**3.** military _____

## Study Guide

Read "American Interest in California." Then fill in the comparison chart below to show what people thought about Manifest Destiny.

| Mexican Leaders | U.S. Settlers |
|---|---|
| **4.** | **5.** |

**6.** Read "The Bear Flag Republic." Then fill in the blanks.

A group of farmers and mountain men called the Bears wanted

to _____ against the Mexican government in

California. _____, a U.S. Army officer, advised the

Bears in their plan of revolt. In June 1846, the Bears took control of

the town of _____, the headquarters of part of the

Mexican army in northern California. This event became known as

the _____.

# Vocabulary and Study Guide

## Vocabulary

1. slavery _____

_____

2. treaty _____

3. territory _____

4. armed forces _____

## Study Guide

5. Read "Neighbors at War." Then fill in the blanks below.

Mexico and the United States could not agree on the

_____ between them. In April 1846, the United States

claimed that Mexican _____ crossed into the United

States and attacked U.S. soldiers. In May, President

_____ declared war on Mexico. U.S. Navy ships quickly

captured several _____ on the California coast.

6. Read "California and the War." Then fill in the blanks below.

Generals Stephen Watts _____ and John Fremont

fought several successful battles against Mexican troops in

California. Then Frémont met _____ at Santa Barbara.

She convinced U.S. and Mexican leaders to sign a _____

that ended the fighting in California. This agreement was called

the _____. The war outside California

continued until Mexico and the United States signed the

_____ in 1848.

# Vocabulary and Study Guide
**Vocabulary**

**Down**

1. a person who leaves one country to live in another
2. someone who went to California in 1849 to look for gold
3. a narrow strip of land between two larger pieces of land

**Across**

4. a _____ takes place when lots of people hurry to a place to look for gold

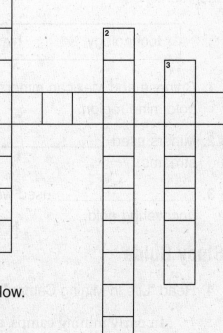

## Study Guide

Read "News of Gold." Then fill in the effects in the chart below.

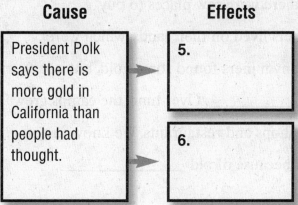

**Cause**

President Polk says there is more gold in California than people had thought.

**Effects**

5.

6.

7. Read "Three Routes." Then fill in the blanks below.

The most popular route to California went across the continent

by _____. The second most popular route took people

to California on _____ that sailed around the tip of

South America. A third route went by sea from the East Coast to

_____. Riverboats and mules crossed the

_____ there. Then a ship took passengers through the

_____ Ocean to California.

# Vocabulary and Study Guide

## Vocabulary

Write the vocabulary word from the box that best completes
each sentence.

| technology | hydraulic mining | discrimination |
|---|---|---|

1. Chinese and Mexican miners faced _____ in California's gold mine region.

2. Miners used _____ to separate sand from gold in streams.

3. _____ used water to wash away hillsides in the hope of uncovering gold.

## Study Guide

4. Read "Life in Mining Camps." Then fill in the blanks below.

In early mining camps, there were few places to buy

_____. Most miners lived on their lands, which were

called _____. Many miners found some gold, but not

enough to make them _____. Over time, the camps grew

into _____ with shops and restaurants. We know about

life in the Gold Rush region because of old _____,

journals, and letters.

**32**   Use with *California Studies*, pp. 178–181

# Skillbuilder: Understand Point of View

| Writer A | Writer B |
|---|---|
| My family lives on a large ranch near Monterey. The land is beautiful, and we have a comfortable life. The Mexican government supports us, but we run our own local affairs. We worry about the U.S. settlers who are now coming here. Some of them do not respect our laws. | I made a long and dangerous journey to get to California. It is a beautiful country. I want to stay here, but the laws are unfair. I think U.S. settlers have the right to spread across this continent. It would be foolish to let the Mexican government stand in our way. California must be part of the United States—and soon! |

## Practice

**1.** What is the point of view of Writer A?

_____

_____

**2.** What words tell you the point of view of Writer A?

_____

_____

_____

_____

**3.** What is the point of view of Writer B?

_____

_____

## Apply

**4.** Write a short paragraph that describes your point of view of California's climate. At the end of your paragraph, describe one or two experiences that have influenced your point of view.

_____

_____

_____

# Vocabulary and Study Guide

## Vocabulary

Write the vocabulary word from the box that best completes the sentence.

| profit | consumer | supply | entrepreneur |
|---|---|---|---|

1. Each miner became a _____ who bought food and other goods.

2. California farmers grew more crops to increase the _____ of food.

3. Levi Strauss was an _____ who made the first blue jeans.

4. Hoping to make a huge _____, people rushed to California to find gold.

## Study Guide

5. Read "Gold Rush Entrepreneurs." Then fill in the blanks below.

   Many entrepreneurs started _____ to serve gold

   miners. Levi Strauss made popular work pants called

   _____. Luzena Stanley Wilson built a _____

   for miners in Nevada City. Domenico Ghirardelli started a company

   that became known for its _____ candy. Lucy Stoddard

   Wakefield sold _____ to miners for $1.00 each.

Read "Gold Rush Entrepreneurs." Then fill in the chart below.

### Entrepreneurs

| Male | Female |
|---|---|
| 6. | 7. |

# Vocabulary and Study Guide

## Vocabulary

Read each definition below. Then write the word that goes with it in the blank.

| convention | delegate | compromise |
| --- | --- | --- |

**1.** an agreement that gives something to both sides _____

**2.** a meeting that brings people together for a common purpose

_____

**3.** a representative chosen to speak or act for others _____

## Study Guide

Read "A Constitutional Convention." Then fill in the chart below.

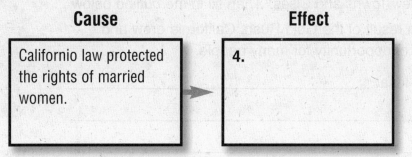

**Cause**

Californio law protected the rights of married women.

**Effect**

4.

**5.** Read "Statehood." Then fill in the blanks.

After they wrote the California constitution, the

_____ petitioned the U.S. Congress for statehood. Until

then, the number of free and slave states was _____.

The _____ worried that a majority of free states would

vote to outlaw slavery. In 1850, the free and slave states reached

a _____ that gave each group something they wanted.

California entered the Union as a _____ state. Southern

states got a _____ against helping slaves escape to free

states.

***Practice Book***
**35**   Use with *California Studies*, pp. 198–203

# Vocabulary and Study Guide

## Vocabulary

Write the definition of each vocabulary word below.

**1.** justice _____

**2.** vigilantes _____

Use each word in a sentence about the lesson.

**3.** _____

_____

**4.** _____

_____

## Study Guide

**5.** Read the chapter "New Towns and Cities." Then fill in the outline below.

**I.** Main Idea: As a result of the Gold Rush, California grew and became a land of opportunity for many people.

**A.** Supporting Idea: _____

_____

**1.** Detail: _____

_____

**2.** Detail: _____

_____

_____

**B.** Supporting Idea: _____

_____

**1.** Detail: _____

_____

**2.** Detail: _____

_____

# Skillbuilder: Interpret Historical Images

## Practice

Use the photograph to answer these questions.

**1.** What is a historical image?

_____

_____

**2.** Is it more likely that this picture of San Francisco is from 1830 or 1850? Explain your answer.

_____

_____

_____

**3.** What are some uses of historical images?

_____

_____

## Apply

**4.** Find an old picture that shows the way a part of your community looked years ago. Check family photos or the library. Then take a picture of that same area today. Write a brief paragraph that compares the way the area looks today with the way it looked in the past. Display your pictures in class. Discuss the changes in your community that the pictures show.

# Vocabulary and Study Guide

## Vocabulary

Write the definition of each vocabulary word below.

**1.** squatter _____

**2.** commission _____

**3.** property right _____

**4.** reservation _____

## Study Guide

**5.** Read "Land Rights." Then fill in the outline below.

   **I.** Main Idea: Different groups of people experienced disputes over land rights in California.

      **A.** Supporting Idea: _____

         _____

         **1.** Detail: _____

           _____

         **2.** Detail: _____

           _____

           _____

      **B.** Supporting Idea: _____

         _____

         _____

         **1.** Detail: _____

           _____

           _____

         **2.** Detail: _____

           _____

Use with *California Studies,* pp. 214–217

# Vocabulary and Study Guide

## Vocabulary

Draw a line to connect the word with its definition.

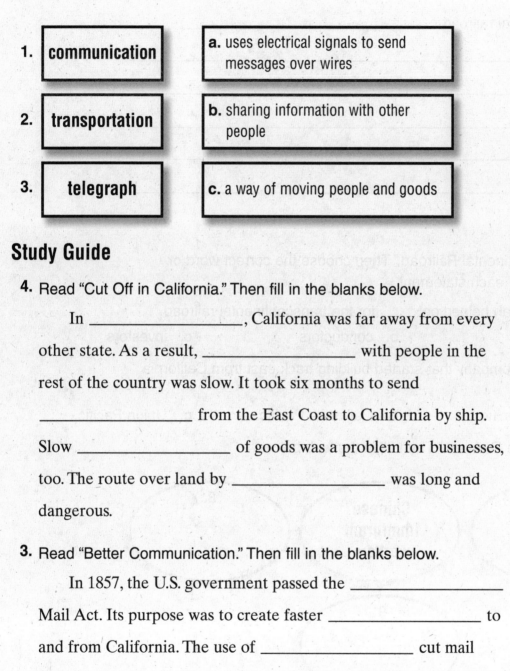

1. communication

2. transportation

3. telegraph

a. uses electrical signals to send messages over wires

b. sharing information with other people

c. a way of moving people and goods

## Study Guide

4. Read "Cut Off in California." Then fill in the blanks below.

In _____, California was far away from every

other state. As a result, _____ with people in the

rest of the country was slow. It took six months to send

_____ from the East Coast to California by ship.

Slow _____ of goods was a problem for businesses,

too. The route over land by _____ was long and

dangerous.

3. Read "Better Communication." Then fill in the blanks below.

In 1857, the U.S. government passed the _____

Mail Act. Its purpose was to create faster _____ to

and from California. The use of _____ cut mail

delivery time to just 25 days. Between 1860 and 1861, the riders of

the _____ cut the time for mail delivery to just ten

days. In 1861, the _____ sent messages on wires

from the rest of the United States to California in just minutes.

# Vocabulary and Study Guide

## Vocabulary

Write the definition of each vocabulary word below.

1. transcontinental railroad _____

2. investor _____

_____

3. engineer _____

4. strike _____

_____

## Study Guide

Read "A Transcontinental Railroad." Then choose the correct word or words to complete each statement.

5. Theodore Judah helped get ＿＿ for the transcontinental railroad.

   **a.** engineers          **b.** conductors          **c.** investors

6. The railroad company that started building track east from California was the

   **a.** Central Pacific.    **b.** California Pacific.    **c.** Union Pacific.

Read "Building the Railroad." Then fill in the web below.

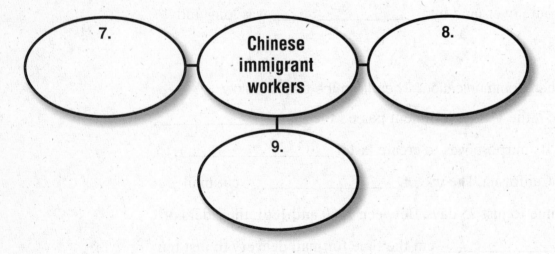

7.

**Chinese immigrant workers**

8.

9.

# Skillbuilder: Distinguish Fact from Opinion

> The opening of the first transcontinental railroad line was the most important event in the history of California. California was isolated before the railroad. It took months for people and goods to travel from the East Coast to California. The worst problem, however, was the slowness of mail. Theodore Judah helped fix that problem by getting investors together for a transcontinental railroad. The federal government further helped by passing the Pacific Railway Act. The Central Pacific started in California and began building the railroad toward the east. The Union Pacific began in the east and headed west. The Central Pacific had the more difficult job and deserves most of the credit.

## Practice

**1.** What are some facts in the passage above?

_____

_____

_____

_____

**2.** What words or phrases show that the author is expressing opinions?

_____

**3.** How does the writer feel about the transcontinental railroad?

_____

_____

## Apply

Do you agree with the author about the transcontinental railroad? Write your own opinion statement about the railroad below.

_____

_____

**Use with** *California Studies*, **pp. 240–241**

# Almanac Map Practice

**INDUSTRY AND RESOURCES**

**LEGEND**

| | | | |
|---|---|---|---|
| Beef cattle | | Oil and gas | |
| Wheat | | Shipbuilding | |
| Vegetables | | Entertainment | |
| Sugar beets | | Aircraft | |
| Cotton | | Forest products | |
| Oranges | | Railroad | |
| Grapes | | Irrigated land | |
| Walnuts | | Major city (over 25,000 people) | |
| Canned foods | | Major canal | |

Use the map to do these activities and answer these questions.

## Practice

**1.** Look at the legend. What does the cow symbol stand for? _____

**2.** What product or industry is found near San Diego? _____

**3.** Which cities have shipbuilding as an industry?

_____

**4.** Which crop is grown near Fresno? _____

## Apply

With a partner, discuss the following: If you were a crop farmer, but also wanted to be near a major city, where would you want to live? Why?

_____

_____

_____

**Use with *California Studies*, p. 248**

Name _____ Date _____

# Almanac Graph Practice

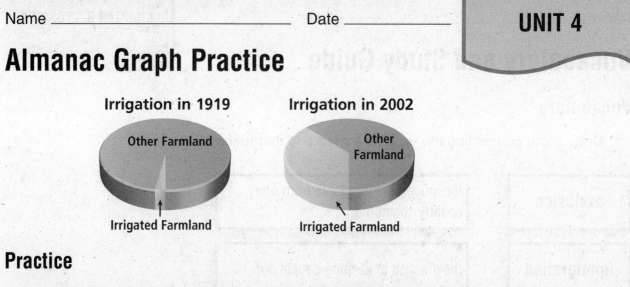

**Irrigation in 1919**

Other Farmland

Irrigated Farmland

**Irrigation in 2002**

Other Farmland

Irrigated Farmland

## Practice

**1.** In which year was more land irrigated, 1919 or 2002?

_____

**2.** What is one reason there might have been more irrigation in that year?

_____

## Apply

**3.** Read the paragraph below. Then use the information to complete the bar graph.

In the United States in 2000, there were a total of 6,653,000 people who had construction jobs. The number of workers with retail jobs, such as those who work in stores, was 23,337,000. There were a total of 40,457,000 people who had jobs in the service industry. The total number of people working in government was 20,702,000.

**U.S. Workers, 2000**

Number of Workers (in millions)

50
40
30
20
10
0

Government   Retail   Construction   Service

**Year**

# Vocabulary and Study Guide

## Vocabulary

**1.** Draw a line connecting the vocabulary word to its meaning.

| exclusion | | the movement of people from one country to another |
|---|---|---|
| immigration | | the practice of keeping people out |

Use one word in a sentence about the lesson.

**2.** _____

_____

## Study Guide

**3.** Read "A New Start." Then fill in the outline below.

   **I.** Main Idea: Mexicans and African Americans contributed to California's economy.

      **A.** Supporting Idea: _____

         _____

         **1.** Detail: _____

           _____

         **2.** Detail: _____

           _____

      **B.** Supporting Idea: _____

         _____

         **1.** Detail: _____

           _____

         **2.** Detail: _____

           _____

*Practice Book*
**44** Use with *California Studies*, pp. 252–257

# Vocabulary and Study Guide

## Vocabulary

Write the definition of each vocabulary word below.

1. irrigation _____

2. migrant worker _____

_____

3. demand _____

_____

4. market _____

Choose two words. Use each word in a sentence about the lesson.

5. _____

_____

6. _____

_____

## Study Guide

7. Read the lesson "California Farming." Then write the names of crops grown in California in the chart below.

8. Read "Railroads and the Market." Then fill in the blanks below.

| **Central Valley** |
|---|
| |

By 1900, there was a growing _____ for fresh produce from California. _____ carried California's crops to distant markets. Railroad cars at first used _____ to keep fruit cold. They were also known as _____ cars. Now people all over the _____ could enjoy fresh fruits and vegetables.

Use with *California Studies*, pp. 260–265

# Vocabulary and Study Guide

## Vocabulary

Write the definition of each vocabulary word below.

**1.** aqueduct _____

_____

**2.** reservoir _____

**3.** hydroelectric power _____

_____

Use each word in a sentence about the lesson.

**4.** _____

_____

**5.** _____

_____

**6.** _____

_____

## Study Guide

**7.** Read "Water for Los Angeles." Then fill in the chart below to show the order or sequence of events of Los Angeles's demand for water.

| 1 | |
|---|---|
| 2 | |
| 3 | |
| 4 | |
| 5 | |

Use with *California Studies*, pp. 268–271

# Skillbuilder: Summarize

In the late 1800s and early 1900s, people moved to California to find land and work. They left their old countries to escape war and crop failures. A large number of them were Asian, Mexican, or African American. The Chinese Exclusion Act of 1882 prevented Chinese people from immigrating to the United States. Although many of these immigrants faced discrimination, they helped the state's economy. California became a leading producer of fruits and vegetables. The money made from agriculture helped Los Angeles and other cities become large and successful.

## Practice

**1.** What are some reasons people immigrated to California?

_____

_____

**2.** How were the Chinese affected by the Chinese Exclusion Act?

_____

_____

_____

**3.** What agricultural products does California specialize in?

_____

## Apply

**4.** Read "Railroads and the Market" in Lesson 2. Then write a summary about crops and the railroad in California.

_____

_____

_____

_____

_____

_____

**47**

# Vocabulary and Study Guide

## Vocabulary

Read the clue and write the answer in the blank. Then circle the word in the puzzle. Look up, down, forward and backward. Look for a bonus word.

1. A community where artists live, work, and learn together is called an artist _____

2. _____ is the way in which something is built.

## Study Guide

3. Read "A Growing City." Then fill in the blanks below.

   During the Gold Rush, thousands of people went to _____ to live. The city was on a huge, natural _____ that made it a successful trade center. In 1869, the _____ _____ reached the area, making travel easy. In 1873, the first _____ _____ line in the United States was built there. The city also had the tallest _____ on the West Coast.

```
A  N  C  O  L  O  N  Y
N  C  I  O  O  C  A  R
E  O  N  N  C  A  D  C
D  N  I  L  S  I  A  D
L  S  E  T  O  N  O  O
U  T  T  B  O  B  R  B
I  R  Y  E  T  T  L  R
N  U  R  R  R  C  I  O
D  C  S  I  C  O  A  C
O  T  B  O  A  C  R  O
C  I  E  C  N  I  C  T
C  O  C  S  R  C  L  N
O  N  C  R  L  N  N  N
```

Read "The Earthquake." Then choose the best ending to each statement below.

4. Much of San Francisco caught fire because of

   ____ **a.** the collapse of wooden buildings.

   ____ **b.** broken water pipes.

   ____ **c.** natural gas ignited by sparks.

5. Many buildings collapsed during the earthquake due to

   ____ **a.** poor construction.

   ____ **b.** empty fire hydrants.

   ____ **c.** cable car accidents.

Use with *California Studies*, pp. 278–281

# Skillbuilder: Identify Primary and Secondary Sources

Read the following passages, and then answer the questions below.

> Some people became rich during or after the Gold Rush. They settled in a neighborhood called Nob Hill. Artists would come to sell their paintings to the rich people. Many of these artists lived together in communities called artist colonies. Artists could work and learn together in the colonies.

> I am very proud of my paintings. My fellow artists and I live together in a community where we can support and learn from each other. I go into Nob Hill every day to sell my paintings to the rich. There is much competition between other artists and myself. There is one particular family that buys many of my paintings.

## Practice

**1.** Which passage is the primary source?

_____

**2.** How do you know this is the primary source?

_____

_____

## Apply

Why do you think reading both primary and secondary sources are important when studying history?

_____

_____

_____

_____

# Vocabulary and Study Guide

## Vocabulary

Write the definition of each vocabulary word below.

**1.** bribe _____

_____

**2.** reform _____

**3.** suffrage _____

Use each word in a sentence about the lesson.

**4.** _____

_____

**5.** _____

_____

**6.** _____

_____

## Study Guide

Read "Cleaning Up State Government." Then fill in the sequence chart below.

**7.**

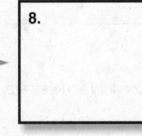
**8.**

Voters gained the power to remove people from elected offices.

**9.** Read "Women Work for Change." Then fill in the blanks below.

In 1909, Katherine Philips Edson led the fight for "_____

_____." She also fought for the right of women to vote, or

_____. Her other causes included providing a minimum

_____ for women and children and reducing working hours for

women to _____ hours a day.

Use with *California Studies*, pp. 290–293

# Vocabulary and Study Guide

## Vocabulary

Write the definition of each vocabulary word below.

**1.** industry _____

_____

**2.** tourism _____

_____

Use each word in a sentence about the lesson.

**3.** _____

_____

**4.** _____

_____

## Study Guide

Read "Effects of World War I." Then choose the correct ending to the statements below.

**5.** Louis B. Mayer, a theater owner, moved to California and started a(n)

____ **a.** movie studio.

____ **b.** airplane factory.

____ **c.** clothing company.

**6.** People grew more cotton in

____ **a.** Death Valley.

____ **b.** the San Diego Valley.

____ **c.** the San Joaquin Valley.

Read "The 1920s." Then choose the correct ending to the statement below.

**7.** The 1920s was a time of

____ **a.** war and peace.

____ **b.** economic growth.

____ **c.** supply shortage.

Use with *California Studies*, pp. 296–299

# Skillbuilder: Read a Circle Graph

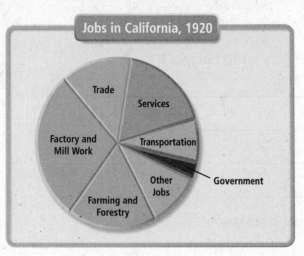

Jobs in California, 1920

## Practice

1. Did more Californians work for the government or work in trade? _____

2. What two categories have almost the same amount of workers?

   _____

3. Circle the category that has the most workers. Why do you think this category had the most workers in 1920? _____

   _____

   _____

## Apply

Create a circle graph to show how much time you spend doing certain activities in a particular day, such as sleeping, going to school, spending time with friends, eating, doing homework, or taking part in an activity. Draw a circle and then divide it into sections to show how you spend your time.

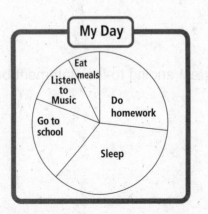

My Day

# Vocabulary and Study Guide

## Vocabulary

If you do not know a word's meaning, try breaking it into smaller parts. It may contain a smaller word that you know.

Find the smaller words inside these words. Use what you know about the smaller word or words to write the meaning of the longer word.

| New Word | Words in it that I know | Word meanings that I know | What I think the word means |
|---|---|---|---|
| **1.** unemployment | | | |

Write the definition of the vocabulary word below.

**2.** depression _____

_____

**3.** drought _____

**4.** unemployment _____

Choose two vocabulary words. Use each in a sentence about the lesson.

## Study Guide

Read "The New Deal." Then fill in the effects in the chart.

**Cause**                                  **Effects**

| President Roosevelt's New Deal is put into action. | → | **5.** |
| | → | **6.** |

# Almanac Map Practice

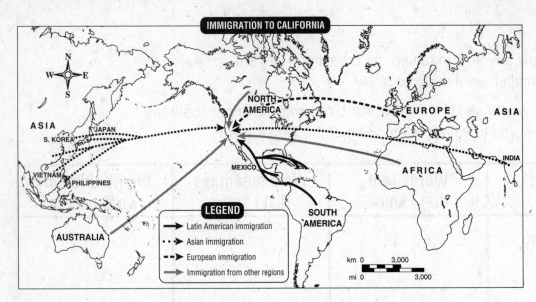

IMMIGRATION TO CALIFORNIA

LEGEND
→ Latin American immigration
••▸ Asian immigration
╌╌▸ European immigration
→ Immigration from other regions

km 0    3,000
mi 0    3,000

Use the map to do these activities and answer these questions.

## Practice

1. How many different categories of immigration are shown in the
   legend? _____

2. In the legend, under which category would you find immigration from

   Africa? _____

3. What is the continent from which most immigrants to California came?

   _____

4. Immigrants from India come from which continent? _____

5. Using the map, how would you describe immigration to California?

   _____

## Apply

6. With a partner, discuss immigration from Latin America to California.

   Describe the arrows or patterns on the map. _____

   _____

   _____

# Almanac Graph Practice

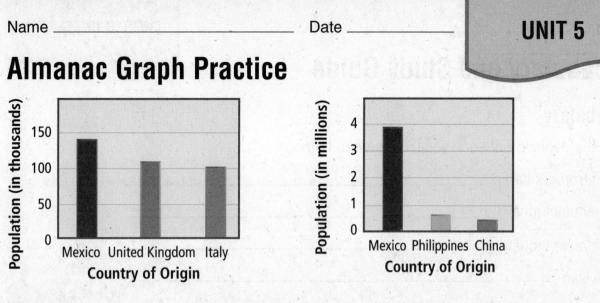

## Practice

1. In 1940 how many Californians were born in Mexico? _____

2. The smallest population of people who moved to California in 2002

   came from which country? _____

## Apply

3. Use the information below to complete the line graph.

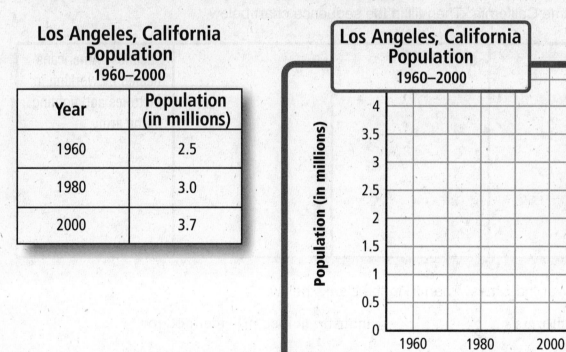

**Los Angeles, California Population 1960–2000**

| Year | Population (in millions) |
|------|--------------------------|
| 1960 | 2.5 |
| 1980 | 3.0 |
| 2000 | 3.7 |

**Los Angeles, California Population 1960–2000**

# Vocabulary and Study Guide

## Vocabulary

Write the definition of each vocabulary word below.

**1.** internment camp _____

**2.** manufacturing _____

**3.** defense industry _____

**4.** civilian _____

Choose two words. Use each in a sentence about the lesson.

**5.** _____

_____

**6.** _____

_____

## Study Guide

Read "Wartime California." Then fill in the sequence chart below.

| 7. | 8. | 9. | Japanese Americans helped by working in factories and fighting in the army. |
|---|---|---|---|
|   |   |   |   |

**10.** Read "War Industries." Then fill in the blanks below.

California's _____ industry helped provide food for

the nation during the war. Many _____ in the state were

used to train troops. _____ also helped the war effort by

manufacturing weapons and other supplies. African Americans,

Mexican Americans, and _____ worked in the factories.

Use with *California Studies*, pp. 320–325

# Skillbuilder: Use a Special Purpose Map

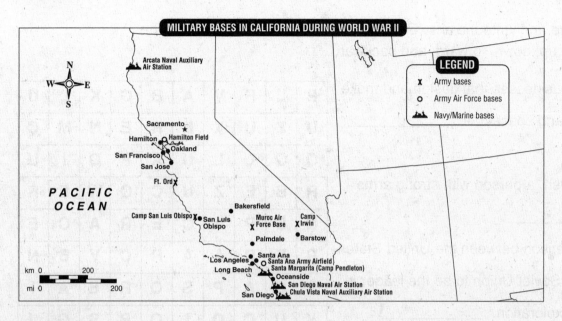

**MILITARY BASES IN CALIFORNIA DURING WORLD WAR II**

LEGEND
X   Army bases
O   Army Air Force bases
⛰   Navy/Marine bases

## Practice

**1.** Look at the map legend. What is the symbol for an army base? _____

**2.** Identify the base that is farthest east. _____

**3.** What are two military bases not located near California's coastline?

_____

_____

## Apply

Read about California's role in World War II in "War Industries." Study the map with a partner. Then discuss ways in which California played an important role in helping the United States win the war.

_____

_____

_____

_____

57    Use with *California Studies,* pp. 330–331

# Vocabulary and Study Guide

## Vocabulary

Read the clue and write the answer in the blank. Then find the word in the puzzle. Look up, down, forward, and backward.

1. All the businesses that design and make rockets and spacecraft. _____ industry

2. In Spanish, a person with strong arms. _____

3. A competition between the United States and the Soviet Union to be the leader in space exploration. _____

| P | L | R | V | A | B | G | K | L | U |
|---|---|---|---|---|---|---|---|---|---|
| U | Z | U | X | E | R | E | N | M | C |
| O | Q | L | L | U | A | P | O | I | U |
| R | B | E | Z | U | C | Q | W | E | R |
| G | S | P | A | C | E | R | A | C | E |
| R | E | D | A | A | R | C | V | B | N |
| E | C | A | P | S | O | R | E | A | I |
| Y | U | C | O | I | O | B | S | G | J |

## Study Guide

Read "Defense and Space Industries." Then fill in the web below to identify jobs connected to California industry.

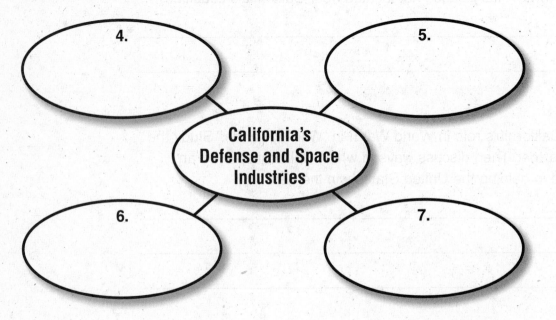

# Vocabulary and Study Guide

## Vocabulary

Write the definition of each vocabulary word below.

**1.** suburb _____

**2.** barrio _____

**3.** pollution _____

**4.** smog _____

Choose two words. Use each in a sentence about the lesson.

**5.** _____

_____

**6.** _____

_____

## Study Guide

Read "Life in the 1950s." Then fill in the sequence chart below to show what happened after World War II.

| | | |
|---|---|---|
| **7.** | **8.** | **9.** |

**10.** Read "Transportation and Entertainment." Then fill in the blanks below.

People in California used _____ to travel between the suburbs and their jobs in the city. Gases and chemicals from cars and factories polluted the air in Los Angeles and created _____. People settled into their new homes and bought _____ for entertainment. Walt Disney created _____ that appealed to the whole family.

Use with *California Studies*, pp. 338–341

# Vocabulary and Study Guide

## Vocabulary

**Across**

1. a refusal to buy, sell, or use certain goods
3. _____ protest is a way to bring change without using violence.
4. the practice of keeping different groups of people separate

**Down**

2. rights that countries guarantee their citizens

## Study Guide

Read "A Call for Equality." Then read the description. In the box, write the name of the person described.

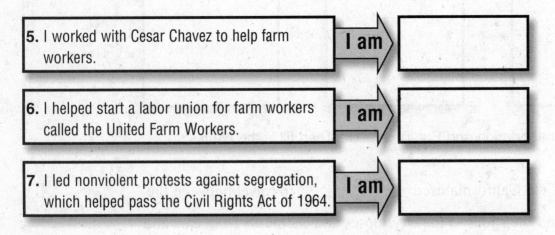

5. I worked with Cesar Chavez to help farm workers. | I am ➤

6. I helped start a labor union for farm workers called the United Farm Workers. | I am ➤

7. I led nonviolent protests against segregation, which helped pass the Civil Rights Act of 1964. | I am ➤

# Vocabulary and Study Guide

## Vocabulary

Read the definitions below. Then write the word that goes with it in the box.

| | |
|---|---|
| **1.** someone who was not born a United States citizen but becomes one | |
| **2.** a person who flees war or danger to find safety some place else | |
| **3.** a person who has special knowledge and training | |

## Study Guide

**4.** Read "From Around the World." Then answer the question.

How did the 1965 immigration laws change immigration patterns from Mexico?

_____

_____

**5.** Read "Coming from Asia." Then answer the question.

What impact did the Vietnam War make on immigration to California?

_____

_____

**6.** Read "Life in the United States." Then answer the question.

How does a person who was not born in the United States become a U.S. citizen?

_____

_____

# Vocabulary and Study Guide

## Vocabulary

**1.** Draw a line connecting the vocabulary word to its meaning.

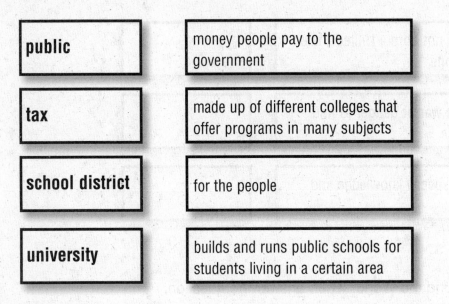

| public | money people pay to the government |
| tax | made up of different colleges that offer programs in many subjects |
| school district | for the people |
| university | builds and runs public schools for students living in a certain area |

## Study Guide

**2.** Read "Education for All." Then answer the question.

How did John Swett propose to pay for the costs of building and running California's public schools?

_____

**3.** Read "The University System." Then answer the question.

How do researchers at colleges and universities help society?

_____

**4.** Read "The University System." Then fill in the blanks.

California's public schools include colleges and

_____. Many students attend two-year programs

at _____ colleges. The state's grant program can help

Californians pay for _____ and fees for college.

California's public school system educates citizens who make

the _____ strong.

# Vocabulary and Study Guide

## Vocabulary

Write the definition of each vocabulary word below.

**1.** high tech _____

_____

**2.** international trade _____

Use each word in a sentence about the lesson.

**3.** _____

_____

**4.** _____

_____

## Study Guide

Read "Leading the Computer Industry." Then fill in the chart below with facts about each area.

| Silicon Valley | The Tech Coast |
|---|---|
| **5.** | **6.** |

**7.** Read "Trade Around the World." Then fill in the blanks.

About 3,000 _____ arrive at the Port of Los Angeles each

year. California companies trade with _____nations that

have coastlines on the Pacific Ocean. The United States, Canada,

and Mexico trade easier with each other because they signed

_____. California helped make trade faster and cheaper by

opening the_____ .

*Practice Book*

**63**    Use with *California Studies*, pp. 370–373

# Vocabulary and Study Guide

## Vocabulary

Write the definition of each vocabulary word below.

**1.** trend _____

**2.** festival _____

Use each word in a sentence about the lesson.

**3.** _____

**4.** _____

_____

## Study Guide

Read "Artists and Trends." Then check the correct ending or answer to each statement below.

**5.** George Lucas is an artist from California who is known for his

____ **a.** paintings.

____ **b.** sculptures.

____ **c.** movies.

**6.** Which band wrote popular songs about California and surfing?

____ **a.** The Beach Boys

____ **b.** The Beatles

____ **c.** The Supremes

**7.** Read "Many Celebrations." Then fill in the blanks below.

Important people honored with holidays in California include

_____ and Cesar Chavez. Customs of the past

are often celebrated at _____. Sometimes people

celebrate _____ such as strawberries and artichokes. The

California State Fair is a week-long festival that celebrates the state's

_____.

# Skillbuilder: Make a Decision

| Decision to Be Made: |
| How to pay for creating and |
| running public schools. |

| Option 1: | Option 2: |
| Use money raised from taxes. | Do not use money from taxes. |

| Final Decision: |

## Practice

1. What are the two options given for how to pay for creating and running public schools? _____

   _____

2. Consider both options. Based on what you read in the chapter, what are the consequences of each?

   _____

   _____

   _____

   _____

3. What was the final decision? Write the decision in the chart.

## Apply

Do you think the final decision was a good one? Why or why not?

_____

_____

_____

_____

# Vocabulary and Study Guide

## Vocabulary

**Down**

1. carries out the nation's laws

**Across**

2. form of government in which power belongs to the people
3. legislates, or makes laws
4. made up of judges and courts that decide what laws mean

## Study Guide

Read "The United States Constitution." Then check the correct ending to each statement below.

5. The purpose and structure of the U.S. government is explained in

____ **a.** the Articles of Confederation.

____ **b.** the Constitution.

____ **c.** the Declaration of Independence.

6. There are three branches of government to

____ **a.** make the President's job harder.

____ **b.** divide and conquer.

____ **c.** limit government power.

7. Read "Rights and Duties." Then fill in the blanks below.

A government in which people elect representatives to make laws is called a

_____. Freedom of speech is a _____ protected by the

Constitution. Citizens have responsibilities that allow them to be part of the

_____. Even if you are too young to _____, you can work to help

your community.

Use with *California Studies*, pp. 388–391

# Skillbuilder: Draw Conclusions

Read the following passage, and then answer the questions below.

The basic law of the United States is the Constitution. According to the Constitution, the government should protect the rights of all citizens. The Constitution divides the national government into three parts, or branches, to make sure that no one group has too much power. Each branch can limit, or check, the power of the other branches. For example, the Supreme Court decides if laws passed by Congress uphold the Constitution. A section of the Constitution called the Bill of Rights protects citizens' rights, such as voting and freedom of speech. Citizens have a duty to obey the law and take part in the government by voting.

## Practice

**1.** What is the topic of the passage?

_____

**2.** What can you conclude about why the Constitution divided the government into three parts?

_____

_____

**3.** What conclusion can you draw about Congress's power to make laws?

_____

_____

_____

## Apply

Study the photograph and read the caption on page 390 of Lesson 1. Use the information to draw a conclusion about how you can be a responsible citizen.

_____

_____

**Use with *California Studies*, pp. 396–397**

# Vocabulary and Study Guide

## Vocabulary

Read the clue and write the answer in the blank. Then find the word in the puzzle. Look up, down, forward, and backward.

1. person who takes care of the daily business of running the city

   _____

2. section of a state that has its own government _____

3. land protected for California Indians _____

| P | L | R | V | A | R | G | K | L | U |
|---|---|---|---|---|---|---|---|---|---|
| U | Z | U | X | E | E | E | N | M | C |
| O | Q | L | L | U | G | P | O | I | U |
| R | B | E | Z | U | A | Q | W | E | R |
| G | S | C | O | U | N | T | Y | C | E |
| R | E | D | A | A | A | C | V | B | N |
| E | C | A | P | S | M | R | E | A | I |
| Y | U | C | O | I | Y | B | S | G | Y |
| O | N | J | A | X | T | L | M | K | P |
| B | G | L | P | Q | I | Z | W | S | H |
| A | I | R | E | H | C | N | A | R | J |

## Study Guide

Read "The Three Branches." Then fill in the web.

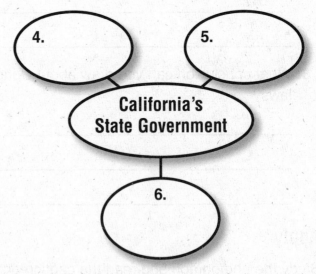

7. Read "Local Government." Then answer the question below.

   What are special districts and what do they do?

   _____

   _____

   _____

# Vocabulary and Study Guide

## Vocabulary

Write the definition of each vocabulary word below.

**1.** population density _____

_____

**2.** metropolitan area _____

_____

**3.** population distribution _____

**4.** service industry _____

_____

## Study Guide

Read "Where Californians Live." Then fill in the chart below to explain why it is important to know about California's population distribution.

| 5. | 6. | 7. |
|---|---|---|
| | | |

**8.** Read "Californians at Work." Then fill in the blanks below.

Californians work in many different _____.

Some work in the _____ industry and have jobs in

hospitals and restaurants. The _____ industry

makes goods such as auto parts and airplanes. Companies that make

cell phones are part of the _____ industry.

Use with *California Studies*, pp. 406–409

# Vocabulary and Study Guide

## Vocabulary

**1.** Draw a line connecting the vocabulary word to its meaning.

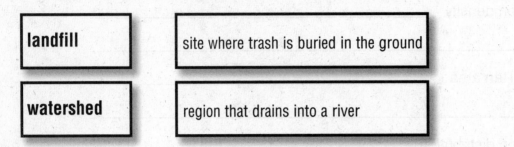

| landfill | site where trash is buried in the ground |
| watershed | region that drains into a river |

## Study Guide

Read "A Great State." Then circle the correct ending to each statement below.

**2.** California leads the United States in many areas and has

  **a.** more people than any other state.

  **b.** the second biggest population of any state.

  **c.** fewer immigrants than any state.

**3.** Air pollution decreased around the country when California

  **a.** limited how many cars people could own.

  **b.** passed laws reducing exhaust from cars.

  **c.** banned cars from interstates and freeways.

**4.** Read "Today's Challenges." Then fill in the blanks below.

California must provide resources for people while still

protecting the _____. One way to help the environment

and lower the amount of trash in landfills is to _____.

People in California also try to save water to protect the

_____. California's _____ will be bright if

everyone tries to solve problems that affect natural resources.

# Skillbuilder: Resolve Conflicts

California's coast is home to many ecosystems, including wetlands, beaches, and bays. Some people want to drill for oil off the shore of California. Oil is an important fossil fuel that is used by many people. The drilling could affect the coast's ecosystems. Other people want to protect the coast's ecosystems and the life they support and to find other sources of energy.

## Practice

**1.** What differences create conflicts about California's coast?

_____

_____

**2.** What are the goals of the people on each side of the conflict?

_____

_____

_____

**3.** What are some possible solutions to this conflict?

_____

_____

_____

## Apply

Think about a conflict in your school. With a partner, discuss the conflict and the goals of each side. Write down possible solutions to the conflict.

_____

_____

_____

_____

**Use with *California Studies*, pp. 418–419**

# Reading Skill and Strategy Practice

# Reading Skill and Strategy

## Reading Skill: Categorize

This skill helps you understand and remember what you have read by organizing facts into groups, or categories.

Read "California's Location." Then fill in the chart below.

### California's Neighbors

| | |
|---|---|
| **1.** North _____ | _____ |
| **2.** South _____ | _____ |
| **3.** East _____ | _____ |
| **4.** West _____ | _____ |

## Reading Strategy: Predict and Infer

**5.** Read "California's Location." Write a prediction about what people from another state might do if they took a vacation to California.

_____

_____

**6.** Read "Geographers Ask Four Questions." What do geographers do?

_____

_____

_____

**7.** Read "Geographers Ask Four Questions." Then write about why geographers ask these questions.

_____

_____

_____

*Practice Book*
3

 **SECTION** *RS*

# Reading Skill and Strategy

## Reading Skill: Main Idea and Details

This skill helps you understand events by seeing how they are related.

Read "California's Land." Then fill in the chart below. Write details that support the main idea.

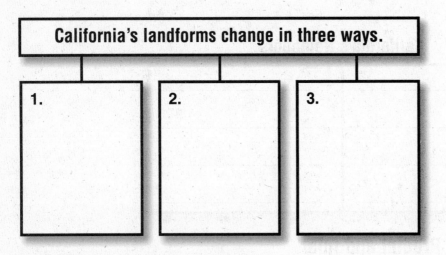

California's landforms change in three ways.

1.

2.

3.

## Reading Strategy: Predict and Infer

Read the following headings in the lesson. Then write what that section of the lesson will be about.

**4.** Changing Landforms

_____

_____

**5.** California's Rivers

_____

_____

**6.** Protecting Land and Water

_____

_____

*Practice Book*
**6**

# Reading Skill and Strategy

## Reading Skill: Compare and Contrast

This skill helps you see how characteristics of something are similar or different.

Read "California's Geographic Regions." Then fill in the Venn diagram below.

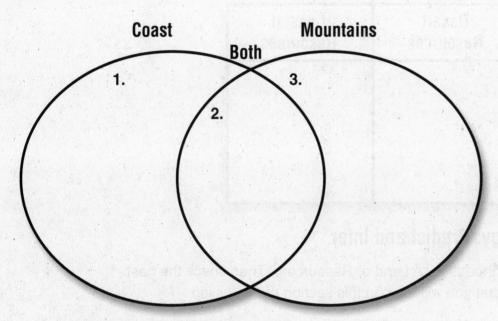

Coast                    Mountains
                  Both
1.                           3.
          2.

## Reading Strategy: Predict and Infer

4. Read "Climate." What can you infer about two places that share the same climate and other features?

   _____

   _____

   _____

5. Read "The Central Valley and Deserts." What can you infer about the Central Valley region?

   _____

   _____

   _____

SECTION **RS**

# Reading Skill and Strategy

## Reading Skill: Categorize

This skill helps you understand and remember what you have read by organizing facts into groups, or categories.

**1.** Read "Desert and Coast Resources." Then fill in the chart below.

| Desert Resources | Coastal Resources |
|---|---|
| | |

## Reading Strategy: Predict and Infer

**2.** Look at the subheads in "A Land of Resources." Then check the best prediction of what you will learn in this section of the lesson.

_____ I will learn how beaches and mountains form.

_____ I will learn about the resources of different parts of California.

_____ I will learn which resources Californians get from other states.

**3.** Look at the pictures in "Using Resources." Use them to predict what the section is about.

_____

_____

**4.** Read "Using Resources." Then check the statement you can infer from this section.

_____ Most resources are nonrenewable.

_____ Renewable resources can become scarce if they are not used wisely.

_____ Steam from the earth is California's most important resource.

# Reading Skill and Strategy

## Reading Skill: Main Idea and Details

This skill helps you understand events by seeing how they are related.

1. Read "California's First People." Then fill in the chart below. Write the main idea.

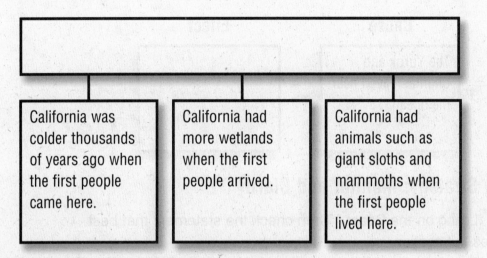

| | | |
|---|---|---|
| California was colder thousands of years ago when the first people came here. | California had more wetlands when the first people arrived. | California had animals such as giant sloths and mammoths when the first people lived here. |

## Reading Strategy: Monitor and Clarify

2. Read "California's First people." Then check the statement that best clarifies the section.

_____ The first people came to California thousands of years ago.

_____ California's first Indians hunted mammoths and giant sloths.

_____ It was colder in California thousands of years ago than it is today.

_____ People have lived in California for millions of years.

3. Read "Different Communities." Then check the statement that best clarifies the section.

_____ About 300,000 people lived in California 500 years ago.

_____ California has mountains, deserts, and beaches.

_____ Hundreds of years ago most Californians lived in towns.

_____ People in different parts of California adapted to different environments.

*Practice Book*
13

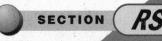

# Reading Skill and Strategy

## Reading Skill: Cause and Effect

This skill helps you see how one event can be related to another, either by causing it or resulting from it.

**1.** Read "Living on the Coast." Then fill in the chart below.

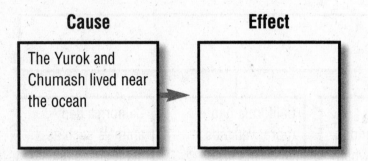

| **Cause** | **Effect** |
| --- | --- |
| The Yurok and Chumash lived near the ocean | |

## Reading Strategy: Monitor and Clarify

**2.** Read "Living on the Coast." Then check the statement that best clarifies the section.

_____ California has deserts and forests along its coast.

_____ California's Indians used many types of coastal resources.

_____ Some resources were common in many parts of California.

Read "Trading Resources." Then complete the statements to clarify why the coastal people traded for goods and services.

**3.** The coastal people had to trade with people in other regions to

_____

Read "Trading Resources." Then fill in the blanks to clarify what trade is.

**4.** When people barter, they _____ resources,

_____, and _____.

# Reading Skill and Strategy

## Reading Skill: Compare and Contrast

This skill helps you see how historical events or people are similar or different.

Read "Valley and Mountain Life." Then complete the chart below.

| Central Valley Life | Sierra Nevada Life |
|---|---|
| 1. | 2. |

## Reading Strategy: Monitor and Clarify

Read "California Indian Religions." Then complete the statement to clarify a reason the Maidu used ceremonies.

3. Ceremonies are formal acts honoring an event or belief. The Maidu

used ceremonies when they danced to _____

_____.

4. Read "California Indian Religions." Then write a sentence that clarifies why traditions are important.

_____

_____

# Reading Skill and Strategy

## Reading Skill: Problem and Solution

This skill helps you see the problems some people faced and how they resolved them.

Read "Adapting to the Desert." Then fill in the chart below.

| Problem | Solution |
|---|---|
| 1. Water was scarce in the desert. | |
| 2. People needed to cool homes in hot summers. | |
| 3. The Mohave needed rich soil to grow crops. | |

## Reading Strategy: Monitor and Clarify

4. Read "Adapting to the Desert." Then clarify the paragraph by writing its main idea below.

> The desert is a hot, dry environment. Some California Indians adapted to life in the desert. They found ways to get scarce water. They used the desert's resources for food and shelter.

_____

_____

# Reading Skill and Strategy

## Reading Skill: Compare and Contrast

This skill helps you understand how historical events or people are similar and different. Read the lesson titled "First Europeans in California." Then fill in the compare and contrast chart below.

| Cabrillo | Drake | Vizcaíno |
|---|---|---|
| 1. | 2. | 3. |

## Reading Strategy: Summarize

4. Read "A Search for Riches." Then check the sentence that best summarizes the section.

_____ European explorers reached California while looking for new trade routes.

_____ European explorers visited many peninsulas and named them after famous kings and queens.

_____ European explorers discovered a short route from Europe to Asia.

5. Read "Exploring the Coast." Then check the sentence that best summarizes the section.

_____ England did not want Spain to colonize any Pacific islands.

_____ The waters along the California coast were very rough.

_____ European explorers carried out expeditions to California in the 1500s.

6. Read "Barriers to Travel." Then check the sentence that best summarizes the section.

_____ A harbor is a place where boats are sheltered from the wind.

_____ It took 150 years for the Spanish to settle in California.

_____ Explorers found it hard to go to California because of wind, mountains, and deserts.

SECTION **RS**

# Reading Skill and Strategy

## Reading Skill: Cause and Effect

This skill helps you see how one event can be related to another, either by causing it or resulting from it.

Read "A Major Expedition." Then fill in the chart below.

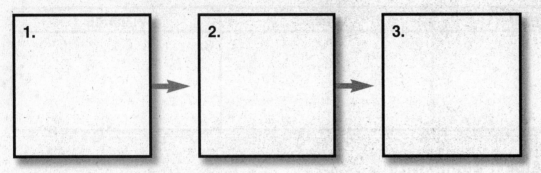

1.

2.

3.

## Reading Strategy: Summarize

4. Read "Seeking New Routes." Then check the sentence that best summarizes the section.

____ James Cook explored the northern Pacific.

____ After Russia and Britain explored the Pacific Ocean, the Spanish planned colonies in California.

____ Vitus Bering worked as an explorer for Russia.

5. Read "A Major Expedition." Then complete the summary.

Catholic priests set up missions to teach others their _____.

# Reading Skill and Strategy

## Reading Skill: Predict Outcomes

This skill allows you to think about what might happen, based on what you have read. Read "A Chain of Missions." Then fill in the predict outcomes chart below.

1.

2.

## Reading Strategy: Summarize

3. Read "A Chain of Missions." Then complete the summary.

   California came under the power of missions set up by Catholics from

   _____.

4. Read "Life on a Mission." Then write a short summary of the section.

   _____

   _____

   _____

5. Read "Resisting the Missions." Then write a short summary of the section.

   _____

   _____

   _____

31    SECTION **RS**

# Reading Skill and Strategy

## Reading Skill: Problem and Solution

This skill helps you see a problem some people faced and how they resolved it.

Read "Presidios and Settlements." Then fill in the chart below.

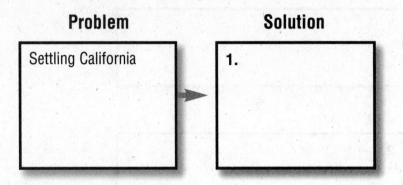

| Problem | Solution |
|---|---|
| Settling California | 1. |

## Reading Strategy: Summarize

**2.** Read "A Growing Colony." Then check the sentence that best summarizes the section.

_____ Juan Bautista de Anza went to Alta California in 1774.

_____ Presidios were built wherever fresh water could be found.

_____ The colony of Alta California was guarded by Spanish soldiers.

_____ Spanish soldiers carried mail along El Camino Real.

**3.** Read "Starting Pueblos." Then write a short summary of the section.

_____

_____

_____

# Reading Skill and Strategy

## Reading Skill: Draw Conclusions

Sometimes when you read, you have to figure out things that the writer doesn't tell you. This skill is called drawing conclusions.

Read "Trade in California." Then complete the chart below.

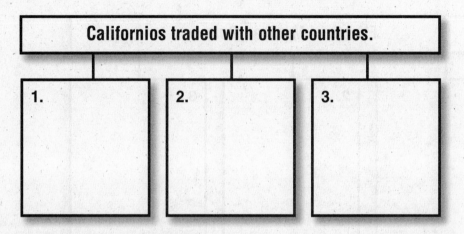

**Californios traded with other countries.**

| 1. | 2. | 3. |

## Reading Strategy: Question

4. Read "Fighting for Freedom." Then check the question that you might ask while reading this section.

_____ Why did people in Alta California want independence from Spain?

_____ Did the people in Spain like the people in New Spain?

_____ Did the king of Spain ever visit Mexico?

5. Read "The Republic of Mexico." Then check the question that you might ask while reading this section.

_____ Why did people in Mexico want an eagle on their flag?

_____ Did Mexico's emperor want to rule any other countries?

_____ Did the new constitution make people in Mexico as free as people in the United States?

6. Read "Trade in California." Then check the question you might ask while reading this section.

_____ How many sea otters did the Aleuts catch?

_____ What color of candles can be made from tallow?

_____ Did Californios get everything they needed by trading goods?

**SECTION** *RS*

# Reading Skill and Strategy

## Reading Skill: Cause and Effect

This skill helps you see how one event can be related to another, either by causing it or resulting from it.

Read the lesson titled "Mexico and California." Then fill in the chart below.

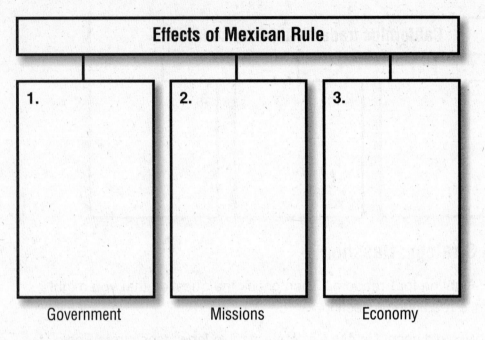

**Effects of Mexican Rule**

1.     2.     3.

Government       Missions       Economy

## Reading Strategy: Question

4. Read "Change in Alta California." Then check the question that you might ask while reading this section.

   ____ Did the Californios want to remain part of Mexico?

   ____ Why did Alta California have a governor?

   ____ How tall were Alta California's mountains?

5. Read "The End of the Missions." Then check the question that you might ask while reading this section.

   ____ Where did the cattle go after the missions closed?

   ____ Were California Indians better off working on the ranchos?

   ____ Were the land grants all the same size?

# Reading Skill and Strategy

## Reading Skill: Compare and Contrast

This skill helps you understand how historical events or people are similar and different. Read the lesson titled "Ranchos and Pueblos." Then fill in the Venn diagram below to compare and contrast ranchos and pueblos.

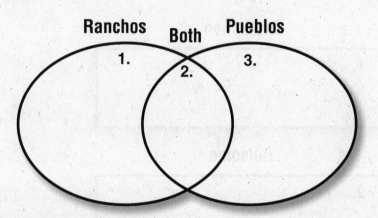

Ranchos  Both  Pueblos

1.

2.

3.

## Reading Strategy: Question

4. Read "The Rise of the Ranchos." Read the answer. Then complete the question for the answer.

   Answer: ranchera

   Question: What is a woman called who owns a _____?

5. Read "Living in a Pueblo." Read the answer. Then complete the question for the answer.

   Answer: alcalde

   Question: What was the title of a person in a pueblo who served as a

   mayor and _____?

6. Read "Living in a Pueblo." Then write two questions to share with a partner.

   _____

   _____

SECTION RS

# Reading Skill and Strategy

## Reading Skill: Predict Outcomes

This skill allows you to think through what might happen, based on what you have read. Read the lesson titled "Trails to California." Then fill in the predict outcomes chart below.

**Prediction**

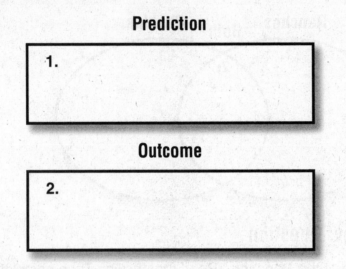

1.

**Outcome**

2.

## Reading Strategy: Question

**3.** Read "Explorers Cross the Frontier." Read the answer. Then complete the question for the answer.

Answer: He was a trapper who was the first American to reach Alta California by land.

Question: Who was _____?

**4.** Read "Pioneers Move West." Read the answer. Then complete the question for the answer.

Answer: They were trapped in snow more than 20 feet deep, and about half of them survived the winter.

Question: Who was _____?

**5.** Read "Sutter's Fort." Read the answer. Then complete the question for the answer.

Answer: He bought Fort Ross from the Russians in 1841.

Question: Who was _____?

# Reading Skill and Strategy

## Reading Skill: Cause and Effect

This skill helps you see how one event can be related to another, either by causing it or resulting from it.

**1.** Read "Bear Flag Revolt." Then fill in the chart below.

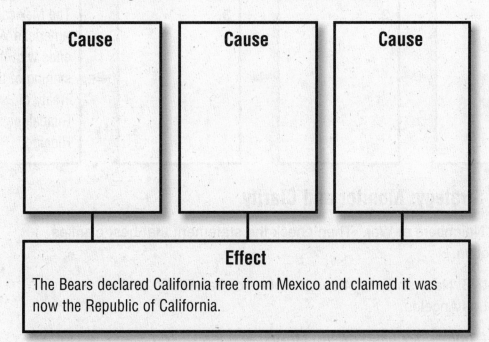

| Cause | Cause | Cause |

**Effect**

The Bears declared California free from Mexico and claimed it was now the Republic of California.

## Reading Strategy: Monitor and Clarify

**2.** Read "American Interest in California." Then check the statement that best clarifies the section.

____ Settlers from the United States did not obey the laws of Mexico.

____ Abel Stearns obeyed the laws of Mexico when he moved to California.

____ Many settlers wanted to make California part of the United States.

**3.** Read "American Interest in California." Then check the statement that best clarifies the section.

____ John C. Frémont advised the Bears on the capture of Sonoma.

____ Some settlers took steps to take California from Mexico.

____ Ezekiel Merritt was one of the leaders in the Bear Flag Revolt.

SECTION **RS**

# Reading Skill and Strategy

## Reading Skill: Sequence

This skill helps you to understand the order in which events happened.

Read "The Mexican-American War." Then fill in the sequence chart below.

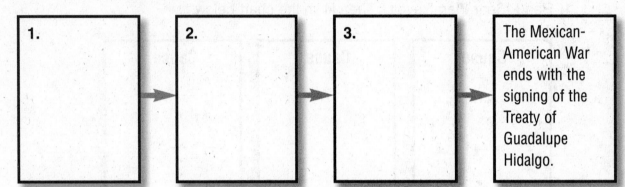

| 1. | 2. | 3. | The Mexican-American War ends with the signing of the Treaty of Guadalupe Hidalgo. |

## Reading Strategy: Monitor and Clarify

4. Read "Neighbors at War." Then check the statement that best clarifies the section.

____ U.S. Navy ships captured the ports of San Diego and Los Angeles.

____ A border dispute between Mexico and the United States led to war.

____ Many Americans believed in Manifest Destiny in the 1800s.

5. Read "California and the War." Then check the statement that best clarifies the section.

____ California became part of the United States after the Mexican-American War.

____ The war ended in 1848 with the signing of the Treaty of Guadalupe Hidalgo.

____ General Stephen Watts Kearney's troops forced some Mexican soldiers to retreat.

# Reading Skill and Strategy

## Reading Skill: Sequence

This skill helps you to understand the order in which events happened.

**1.** Read "News of Gold." Then fill in the sequence chart below.

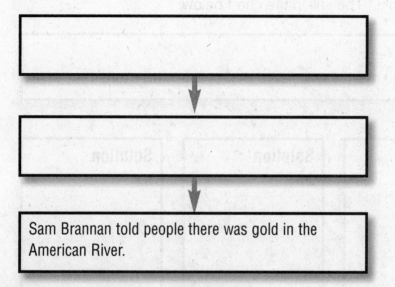

Sam Brannan told people there was gold in the American River.

## Reading Strategy: Monitor and Clarify

**2.** Read "News of Gold." Then explain how the news that gold was discovered spread across the United States.

_____

_____

_____

**3.** Read "Three Routes." Then explain why forty-niners used these routes to get to California.

_____

_____

_____

_____

**SECTION** 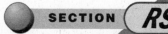 **RS**

# Reading Skill and Strategy

## Reading Skill: Problem and Solution

This skill helps you see what problem some people faced and how they resolved it.

Read "Mining Gold." Then fill in the chart below.

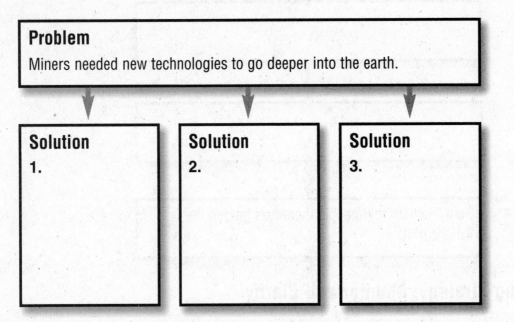

**Problem**
Miners needed new technologies to go deeper into the earth.

**Solution**
1.

**Solution**
2.

**Solution**
3.

## Reading Strategy: Monitor and Clarify

4. Read "Mining Gold." Then tell how you monitored your understanding of the section.

_____

_____

_____

5. Write any questions you had after you finished reading.

_____

_____

_____

_____

# Reading Skill and Strategy

## Reading Skill: Main Idea and Details

This skill helps you understand events by seeing how they are related.

Read "Business Booms." Then fill in the chart below. Write details that support the main idea.

**Main Idea**
Satisfying the needs of miners helped many businesses start and grow.

| Detail 1. | Detail 2. | Detail 3. |
| --- | --- | --- |
| | | |

## Reading Strategy: Question

4. Read "Business Booms." Then check the question that you might ask while reading this section.

_____ What types of food did California farms grow in the 1800s?

_____ What were some new technologies used to search for gold?

_____ What happened to some towns after nearby mines closed?

5. Read "Gold Rush Entrepreneurs." Then check the question that you might ask while reading this section."

_____ Were some of today's businesses started by Gold Rush entrepreneurs?

_____ What techniques did miners use to separate gold from rock and soil?

_____ How many people moved to California during the Gold Rush?

# Reading Skill and Strategy

## Reading Skill: Sequence

This skill helps you to understand the order in which events happened.

Read "The Thirty-first State." Then fill in the sequence chart below.

| | |
|---|---|
| 1. | |
| 2. | |
| 3. | |
| 4. | |

## Reading Strategy: Question

5. Read "Reasons for a State." Then read the answer below. Next, complete the question that would result in this answer.

   **Answer:** Americans in California wanted to vote to choose their leaders.

   **Question:** Why did

   _____

   _____

6. Read "A Constitutional Convention." Then write a question to share with a partner.

   _____

   _____

   _____

7. Read "Statehood." Then write a question to share with a partner.

   _____

   _____

# Reading Skill and Strategy

## Reading Skill: Compare and Contrast

This skill helps you understand how historical events or people are similar and different.

Read "New Towns and Cities." Then complete the chart below.

| Before or at the Start of the Gold Rush | After the Gold Rush |
|---|---|
| 1. Yerba Buena was a small village.<br>2. Mudville was a small muddy mining camp on the San Joaquin River.<br>3. Sacramento was a small port on the Sacramento River. | 1.<br><br>2.<br><br>3. |

## Reading Strategy: Question

4. Read "Building Towns." Then check the question that you might ask while reading this section.

____ How did businesses in Los Angeles grow?

____ How did the Gold Rush change San Francisco?

____ How many miners lived in Nevada City?

____ Why did the Sacramento River flood so often?

5. Read "Seeking Success." Then check the question that you might ask while reading this section.

____ What women created businesses during the Gold Rush?

____ Who started California's first African American newspaper?

____ Who was the most successful gold miner in California?

____ How did California's constitution set up rules for behavior?

Name _____ Date _____

# Reading Skill and Strategy

## Reading Skill: Main Idea and Details

This skill helps you understand events by seeing how they are related.

Read "Californio Lands." Then in the chart below write details that support the main idea.

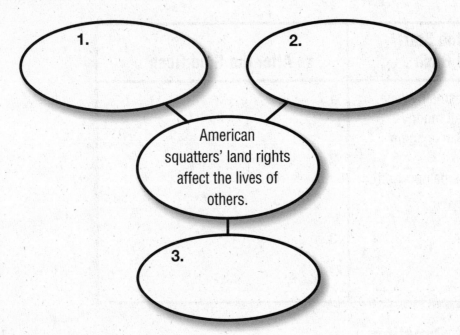

1.

2.

American squatters' land rights affect the lives of others.

3.

## Reading Strategy: Question

4. Read "Californio Lands." Then check the question that you might ask while reading this section.

_____ Why was there conflict between Californios and newcomers?

_____ What steps did people take to make California a state?

_____ Why did Mexico lose the Mexican-American War?

5. Read "Reservations." Then check the question you might ask while reading the section.

_____ How many Indian nations are in California today?

_____ Why did the Modocs fight the U.S. government?

_____ What did Californios think of Indian neighbors?

# Reading Skill and Strategy

## Reading Skill: Problem and Solution

This skill helps you see what problem some people faced and how they resolved it.

**1.** Read "Linking East and West." Then fill in the chart below.

| Problem | Solution |
|---|---|
| It took news and mail many months to get to California. | |

## Reading Strategy: Summarize

**2.** Read "Cut Off in California." Then check the best summary.

_____ The population of California was spread out in 1850.

_____ It was difficult for California to get goods and news.

_____ The land route for wagons was dangerous and long.

**3.** Read "Better Communication." Then check the best summary.

_____ Different types of animals, such as camels and dogs, carried mail to California.

_____ The Pony Express moved mail between California and Missouri in record time.

_____ Faster mail delivery and telegraph messages improved communication with California.

*Practice Book*
**65**

 **SECTION** *RS*

# Reading Skill and Strategy

## Reading Skill: Main Idea and Details

This skill helps you understand events by seeing how they are related.

Read "A Transcontinental Railroad." Then fill in the chart below. Write details that support the main idea.

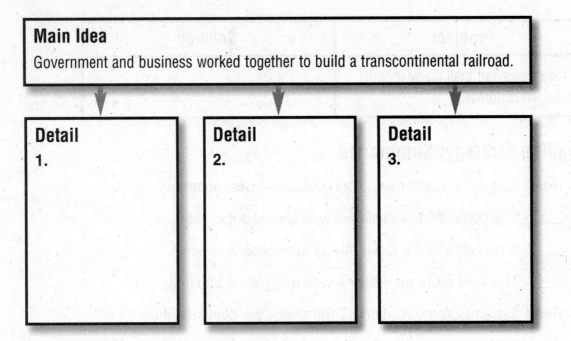

**Main Idea**
Government and business worked together to build a transcontinental railroad.

**Detail 1.**

**Detail 2.**

**Detail 3.**

## Reading Strategy: Summarize

4. Read "Building the Railroad." Then check the sentence that best summarizes the section.

_____ Many laborers worked long and hard on the transcontinental railroad.

_____ Chinese and Irish immigrants were hired to work on the railroad.

_____ The Central Pacific and Union Pacific railroads met in May 1869.

5. Read "Building the Railroad." Then complete the summary.

Many of the people building tracks for the Central Pacific were Chinese immigrants. In June of 1867,

_____

_____

# Reading Skill and Strategy

## Reading Skill: Compare and Contrast

This skill helps you understand and remember what you have read by organizing facts into groups, or categories.

Read "Moving to California." Then complete the chart below.

**Before the Chinese Exclusion Act    After the Chinese Exclusion Act**
**Both**

1.

3.    2.

## Reading Strategy: Summarize

**4.** Read "Moving to California." Then write a summary of the section.

_____

_____

_____

_____

**5.** Read "Farm Workers from Asia." Then write a summary of the section.

_____

_____

_____

_____

_____

 **SECTION** **RS**

# Reading Skill and Strategy

## Reading Skill: Cause and Effect

This skill helps you see how one event can be related to another, either by causing it or resulting from it.

**1.** Read "A Good Place to Farm." Then fill in the chart below.

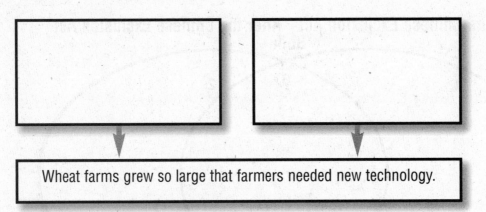

Wheat farms grew so large that farmers needed new technology.

## Reading Strategy: Summarize

**2.** Read "A Good Place to Farm." Then check the statement that best summarizes the section.

_____ Wheat does not spoil easily.

_____ California developed its farmland using new crops and equipment.

_____ The combined harvester made harvesting crops much easier.

**3.** Read "Working the Land." Then check the statement that best summarizes the section.

_____ Irrigation systems and lots of workers helped farms grow.

_____ Young children of migrant workers often helped pick crops.

_____ George Shima was known as the "Potato King."

**4.** Read "Railroads and the Market." Then check the statement that best summarizes the section.

_____ Railroads transported California's crops to distant markets.

_____ Markets are places where goods and services are exchanged.

_____ Irrigation changed farming in California's Central Valley.

# Reading Skill and Strategy

## Reading Skill: Main Idea and Details

This skill helps you understand events by seeing how they are related.

**1.** Read "Los Angeles." Then fill in the idea web below.

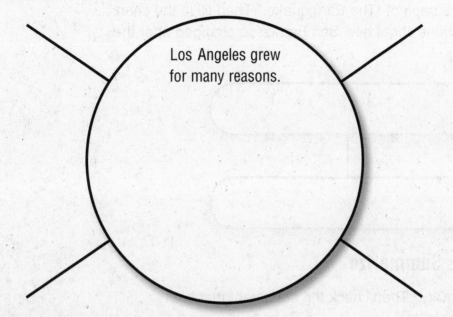

Los Angeles grew
for many reasons.

## Reading Strategy: Summarize

**2.** Read "Better Transportation." Then write a summary of the section.

_____

_____

_____

**3.** Read "Water for Los Angeles." Then write a summary of the section.

_____

_____

_____

**4.** Read the lesson titled "Los Angeles." Then write a summary.

_____

_____

_____

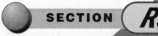

**SECTION** *RS*

# Reading Skill and Strategy

## Reading Skill: Predict Outcomes

This skill allows you to think about what might happen, based on what you have read.

1. Read the first paragraph of "The Earthquake." Then fill in the chart below with predictions about how San Francisco changed after the 1906 earthquake.

## Reading Strategy: Summarize

2. Read "A Growing City." Then check the statement that best summarizes the section.

____ Mills in San Francisco produced flour and lumber.

____ Artist colonies were small communities of artists.

____ San Francisco began growing after the Gold Rush.

____ The first cable cars were used in San Francisco.

3. Read "The Earthquake." Then check the statement that best summarizes the section.

____ The 1906 earthquake broke many of San Francisco's water pipes.

____ San Francisco was badly damaged by the earthquake.

____ There were many horse-drawn carriages used following the earthquake.

____ Due to the earthquake, many people had to live in tents.

# Reading Skill and Strategy

## Reading Skill: Cause and Effect

This skill helps you see how one event can be related to another, either by causing it or resulting from it.

**1.** Read "Cleaning Up State Government." Then complete the chart

| **Cause** | **Effect** |
|---|---|
| San Francisco's mayor and other leaders took bribes to help certain businesses make money.  | |

below.

## Reading Strategy: Predict and Infer

**2.** Read the first paragraph of "Cleaning Up State Government." Then check the best prediction.

_____ The leaders will be more careful when taking bribes.

_____ People will get angry and demand honesty from their leaders.

_____ The leaders will pay the police to forget about the bribes.

_____ People will reelect the leaders in future elections.

**3.** Read "Women Work for Change." Then check the best statement you can infer from this section.

_____ Children should never have to do anything.

_____ Employers like to pay employees as much as they can.

_____ Some women proved that they could make society more fair.

_____ Minimum wage is always enough to live on.

# Reading Skill and Strategy

## Reading Skill: Main Idea and Details

This skill helps you understand events by seeing how they are related.

Read "Effects of World War I." Then fill in the chart below.

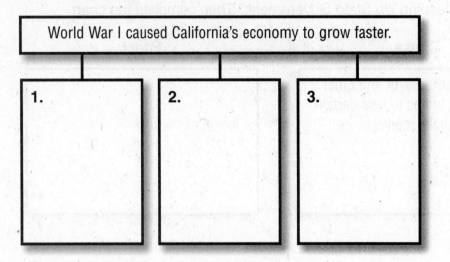

World War I caused California's economy to grow faster.

1.

2.

3.

## Reading Strategy: Predict and Infer

4. Read "Effects of World War I." Then check the best prediction.

_____ Soldiers from California will wear clean uniforms every day.

_____ Once the war is over, people will stop going to movies.

_____ California will run out of crops to feed people after the war.

_____ The money coming into California will help the economy grow.

5. Read "The 1920s." Then complete the statement.

When cars became popular in the 1920s, _____

_____.

# Reading Skill and Strategy

## Reading Skill: Problem and Solution

This skill helps you see what problem some people faced and how they resolved it.

Read "The Great Depression." Then fill in the chart below.

| Problem | Solution |
|---|---|
| **1.** Many people lost their jobs. | |
| **2.** Banks closed during the Depression. | |

## Reading Strategy: Predict and Infer

3. Read the first two paragraphs of "The Depression Years." Then complete the prediction.

   During the Great Depression, many people in California will

   _____

   _____.

4. Read the last paragraph of "The New Deal." Then complete the prediction.

   During his terms in 1936 and 1940, President Roosevelt will

   _____

   _____

   _____.

5. Read "The New Deal." Then make an inference.

   Will the economy pick up again? _____

   _____

   _____

# Reading Skill and Strategy

## Reading Skill: Cause and Effect

This skill helps you see how one event can be related to another, either by causing it or resulting from it.

Read "California and World War II." Then fill in the chart below.

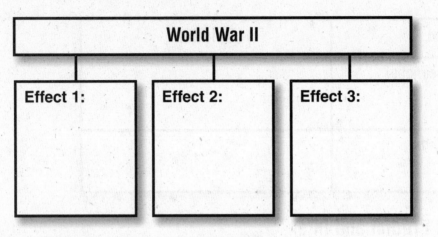

**World War II**

Effect 1:

Effect 2:

Effect 3:

## Reading Strategy: Monitor and Clarify

**4.** Read "Wartime California." Then check the statement that best clarifies the section.

_____ Japanese Americans were held captive in camps during the war.

_____ Many Japanese Americans fought in World War II.

_____ The United States fought against Japan, Germany, and Italy.

**5.** Read "War Industries." Then check the statement that best clarifies the section.

_____ California built more airplanes than any other state.

_____ Many industries, businesses, and people in California worked for the war effort.

_____ Many Californians served in the military during the war.

**6.** Read "Pitching In." Then check the statement that best clarifies the section.

_____ The United States had many civilians.

_____ Americans aided in any way they could during the war.

_____ The United States and its allies won World War II in 1945.

# Reading Skill and Strategy

## Reading Skill: Main Idea and Details

This skill helps you understand events by seeing how they are related.

Read "Peacetime Industries." Then fill in the chart below. Write the main idea in the large box. Write details that support the main idea in the smaller boxes.

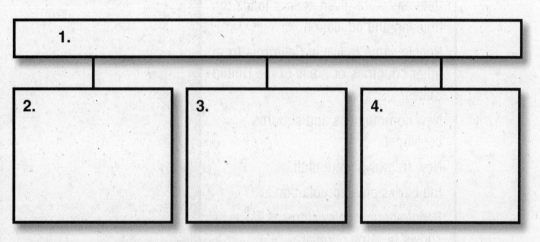

## Reading Strategy: Monitor and Clarify

5. Read "Defense and Space Industries." Then check the statement that best clarifies the section.

    _____ California's defense and aerospace industries grew after World War II.

    _____ The United States and the Soviet Union competed in the space race.

    _____ The Soviet Union made powerful weapons after World War II.

    _____ Scientists in California helped the United States win the space race.

6. Read "The Leading Farm State." Then check the statement that best clarifies the section.

    _____ Machines were developed in California to help farms increase productivity.

    _____ Workers from Mexico called braceros worked on California farms.

    _____ California grew one-third of the country's fruit after World War II.

    _____ California became a leader in agriculture after World War II.

SECTION **RS**

# Reading Skill and Strategy

## Reading Skill: Compare and Contrast

1. Read "Building New Communities." Then complete the chart below.

| Before World War II | After World War II |
|---|---|
| | Veterans were given special loans for housing and education. |
| | People came to live in California from other countries or areas of the United States. |
| | New communities and suburbs developed. |
| | New freeways were built. |
| | Industries created pollution. |
| | People bought televisions as TV shows became popular. |
| | Theme parks were built. |

## Reading Strategy: Monitor and Clarify

2. Read "Life in the 1950s." Then complete the sentence to clarify why people moved into new communities.

People moved into new communities in California because

_____

_____

_____

3. Read "Transportation and Entertainment." Then write a sentence clarifying how televisions changed people's lives.

_____

_____

# Reading Skill and Strategy

## Reading Skill: Problem and Solution

This skill helps you see what problems some people faced and how they resolved them.

Read "A Call for Equality." Then fill in the chart below. Write the problems faced by these groups of people in the boxes on the left. Write their solutions to the problems in the boxes on the right.

| 1. problem: | 2. solutions: |
| --- | --- |

| 3. problem: | 4. solutions: |
| --- | --- |

## Reading Strategy: Monitor and Clarify

5. Read "Civil Rights." Then check the statement that best clarifies the section.

____ In southern states, schools, restaurants, and parks were segregated.

____ Martin Luther King Jr. was a leader in the civil rights movement.

____ People protested discrimination by using forms of nonviolent protest.

____ African Americans fought for civil rights in the 1960s and 1970s.

6. Read "United Farm Workers." Then write a sentence that clarifies how Cesar Chavez helped equality.

_____

_____

_____

# Reading Skill and Strategy

## Reading Skill: Main Idea and Details

This skill helps you understand events by seeing how they are related.

Read "New Neighbors Arrive." Then fill in the chart below.

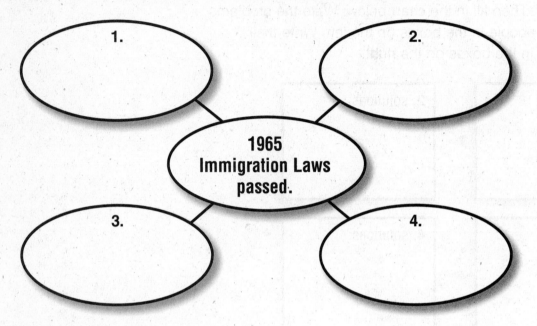

## Reading Strategy: Summarize

5. Read "From Around the World." Then check the statement that best summarizes the section.

____ Workers and professionals immigrated to California in the 1960s.

____ Immigration laws made it easier for people to immigrate to California.

6. Read "Coming from Asia." Then check the statement that best summarizes the section.

____ New immigration laws allowed refugees to come live in the United States.

____ After 1965, immigration to California from Asia increased.

7. Read "Life in the United States." Then complete the summary. Immigrants in California are important to the state and nation because

_____

_____

# Reading Skill and Strategy

## Reading Skill: Categorize

This skill helps you understand and remember what you have read by organizing facts into groups, or categories.

**1.** Read "Education in California." Then fill in the chart below.

| Public Schools | University System |
|---|---|
| | |

## Reading Strategy: Summarize

**2.** Read "Education for All." Then check the statement that best summarizes the section.

____ California's public school system is the largest school system in the country.

____ People worked hard to develop a public school system in California.

____ Public schools are funded by taxes that people pay the government.

____ Early public schools in California had only one room for all students.

**3.** Read "The University System." Then check the statement that best summarizes the section.

____ College graduates are needed in California's business offices and factories.

____ California has grant programs that help students pay for college.

____ Universities in California improve health and safety through research.

____ California's public universities and colleges help create educated citizens.

SECTION RS

# Reading Skill and Strategy
## Reading Skill: Draw Conclusions

Sometimes when you read, you have to figure out things that the writer doesn't tell you. This skill is called drawing conclusions.

Read "Technology and Trade." Then fill in the chart with details and facts about the computer industry.

| | |
|---|---|
| 1. | |
| 2. | |
| 3. | |
| 4. | |

5. Think about things the computer industry provides. Do you think one thing is more important than another? Why did you draw that conclusion?

_____

_____

_____

_____

## Reading Strategy: Predict and Infer

6. Read "Leading the Computer Industry." Then check the sentence that best summarizes the section.

____ Industries in Silicon Valley and the Tech Coast make California a leader in high-tech.

____ Silicon Valley is named for silicon chips in computers.

____ Stanford University set up a research park that brought companies to California.

7. Read "Trade Around the World." Then complete the summary. California is a leader in international trade because

_____

_____

# Reading Skill and Strategy

## Reading Skill: Categorize

This skill helps you understand and remember what you have read by organizing facts into groups, or categories.

Read "California's Art and Culture." Then fill in the chart below with different categories of holidays and festivals that are celebrated in California.

| | |
|---|---|
| 1. | |
| 2. | |
| 3. | |
| 4. | |

## Reading Strategy: Summarize

5. Read "Artists and Trends." Then write a summary of the section.

_____

_____

_____

_____

6. Read "Many Celebrations." Then write a summary of the section.

_____

_____

_____

_____

_____

_____

SECTION **RS**

# Reading Skill and Strategy

## Reading Skill: Categorize

This skill helps you understand and remember what you have read by organizing facts into groups, or categories.

Read "United States Government." Then complete the chart. Categorize which people or groups make up each branch of the government.

| Legislative branch | Executive branch | Judicial branch |
|---|---|---|
| 1. | 2. | 3. |

## Reading Strategy: Monitor and Clarify

4. Read "The United States Constitution." Then check the statement that best clarifies the section.

____ The U.S. Constitution was written more than 200 years ago.

____ The Constitution divides the government into three branches to limit power.

____ The purpose of government is to protect the rights of every citizen.

5. Read "Rights and Duties." Then check the statement that best clarifies the section.

____ Citizens in a democracy like the United States have rights and responsibilities.

____ Voting is a right and duty that gives citizens real power in government.

____ Students can take part in government by working to change unjust laws.

# Reading Skill and Strategy

## Reading Skill: Compare and Contrast

This skill helps you understand how historical events or people are similar and different.

Read "State and Local Government." Then fill in the chart below.

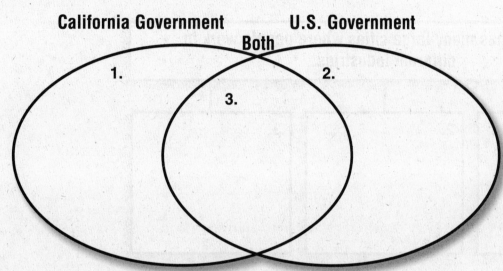

**California Government**    **U.S. Government**
**Both**

1.

2.

3.

## Reading Strategy: Monitor and Clarify

4. Read "State Government." Then check the statement that best clarifies the section.

    ____ California's government, like the national government, is based on a constitution.

    ____ California's government collects state taxes to pay for many services and programs.

5. Read "The Three Branches." Then complete the statement below clarifying the section.

    Like the national government, California's government is divided into

    _____

6. Read "Local Government." Then complete the statement below clarifying the section.

    Local governments in California provide

    _____

    _____

# Reading Skill and Strategy

## Reading Skill: Main Idea and Details

This skill helps you understand events by seeing how they are related.

Read "Californians Today." Then fill in the chart below. Write details that support the main idea.

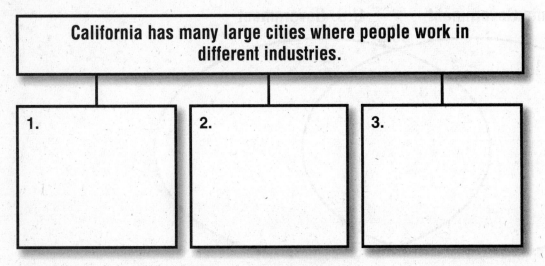

```
┌─────────────────────────────────────────────┐
│   California has many large cities where     │
│   people work in different industries.       │
└─────────────────────────────────────────────┘

┌──────────┐    ┌──────────┐    ┌──────────┐
│ 1.       │    │ 2.       │    │ 3.       │
│          │    │          │    │          │
│          │    │          │    │          │
│          │    │          │    │          │
└──────────┘    └──────────┘    └──────────┘
```

## Reading Strategy: Monitor and Clarify

4. Read "Where Californians Live." Then complete the statement below that clarifies the section.

   Studying changes in California's population distribution is important

   because _____.

5. Read "Californians at Work." Then complete the statement below that clarifies the section.

   Californians choose to work in a variety of industries, such as

   _____

# Reading Skill and Strategy

## Reading Skill: Problem and Solution

This skill helps you see what problems some people faced and how they resolved them.

Read "The Challenge of the Future." Then fill in the chart below describing problems that affect California's environment and solutions to the problems.

| Problem | Solution |
|---------|----------|
| 1. | 4. |
| 2. | 5. |
| 3. | 6. |

## Reading Strategy: Monitor and Clarify

7. Under which heading in Lesson 4 would you find information about

   challenges in California?

   _____

8. Read "A Great State." Then write a question you might have while

   reading the section. _____

   _____

9. How did you answer your question? Answer with a complete

   sentence.

   _____

   _____

   _____

10. Read "Today's Challenges." How can you help the environment?

    _____

    _____

# Interactive Lesson Summaries

# Summary: Where Is California?

## California's Location

We are going to study the geography of our state, California. Geography is the study of people, places, and environments. Environment means parts of nature, such as land, water, and air.

California is one of the fifty states that make up the United States. West of California is the Pacific Ocean. To the north is Oregon. To the south is Mexico. The United States of America is on the continent of North America.

Look at a map or a globe. The point farthest north is the North Pole. The point farthest south is the South Pole. The equator is the imaginary line around the middle of Earth. It is an equal distance from both poles. Earth is divided into two hemispheres. From the equator to the North Pole is the Northern Hemisphere. From the equator to the South Pole is the Southern Hemisphere. California, like the rest of North America, is in the Northern Hemisphere.

## Geographers Ask Four Questions

Geographers are the people who study geography. They ask four major questions about places: (1) Where is it? (2) What is it like there? (3) Why is it there? (4) How do places change? When geographers ask where a place is, they want to know about its location. For example, California is on the Pacific Ocean.

When geographers ask what a place is like, they want to know what physical features it has, such as seashore or mountains. They might also ask questions about the number of people and what kinds of work they do.

When geographers ask why a place is there, they want to understand how different parts of the environment affect each other. Why are plants in northern California different from those in southern parts of the state? They would also want to understand how the land affects people.

When geographers ask how places change, they want to know how places change over time. Human activities and physical forces change landscapes. Natural forces such as storms and earthquakes also change the land.

**Before You Read**

Find and underline each vocabulary word.

**geography** *noun*, the study of places, people, and environments

**continent** *noun*, one of the seven great land areas on Earth

**equator** *noun*, imaginary line around Earth, dividing it into the Northern and Southern hemispheres

**hemisphere** *noun*, one of the two halves of Earth, from the equator to one of the poles

**After You Read**

**REVIEW** The state of California is located in which country, continent, and hemisphere? Highlight the three sentences that give you this information about California.

**REVIEW** Name the four questions that geographers ask and explain what they mean. Draw a box around the paragraph that lists the questions. Then underline the main sentences that describe what geographers want to determine by asking each question.

# Summary: Land and Water

## California's Land

California has many types of landforms, including two large mountain ranges. One, near the coast, is called the Coast Ranges. Most cities and towns are in low-lying parts of these mountains. The other range is the Sierra Nevada. California's largest mountain range is more than 400 miles long. Fewer people live in these mountains than in lower areas. The Sierra Nevada is on the eastern side of the state.

California's landforms have changed in three ways over time. First, volcanoes created many mountains. A volcano is an opening in Earth's surface through which very hot lava, ash, and gas escape. Then, earthquakes also reshape land. Movement of large plates in Earth's crust cause earthquakes. They raise or lower landforms and change the course of rivers.

Third, erosion changes landforms very slowly by wearing them away by wind or water. Over time, erosion creates valleys and canyons out of mountains.

## California's Water

California has rivers, lakes, and ocean bays. People use fresh water for drinking, farming, and fishing. In salt water, people enjoy swimming, surfing, and boating. High in the Sierra Nevada are two lakes partly created by volcanoes. Lake Tahoe is a freshwater lake, but Mono Lake is very salty.

The Colorado River, along the southeastern border of California, is used for farming. The two largest rivers in the state are the Sacramento River and San Joaquin River. They meet and flow into a delta that empties into San Francisco Bay.

California's long coast has hundreds of bays. Some bays have deep harbors for ships. The Port of Los Angeles, in San Pedro harbor, is one of the world's busiest ports.

Californians have worked hard to protect their environment. This is called conservation. People depend on the environment for important things such as food and drinking water.

### Before You Read

Find and underline each vocabulary word.

**landform** *noun*, feature on Earth's surface, such as a valley

**delta** *noun*, flat, triangle-shaped area of land at the mouth of a river

**environment** *noun*, the natural landscape, such as air, water, plants, trees, and mountains

### After You Read

**REVIEW** What are three ways that California's landforms change over time? Forces of nature change landforms over time. Underline the sentences that discuss the three ways landforms change.

**REVIEW** What are the similarities and differences of three bodies of water in California? Fresh water and salt water have different uses. In California, there are lakes, rivers, and bays that supply water. Highlight sentences that give you specific information about this.

# Summary: Climate and Regions

## Climate

Weather is the condition in a place at a particular time, such as rainy, foggy, windy, or sunny weather. Climate is the weather pattern of a region over time. Three things affect climate. Places closer to the equator or near the ocean have warmer climates, but the higher a place, the colder its climate. California has a variety of climates. Areas that share similar climates are called climate regions. Northern California has a temperate, or moderate, climate. Southern California and the Central Valley have a warmer climate with dry summers and rainy winters. The Valley climate makes it possible for farmers to grow crops year round.

## Regions of California

California has four geographic regions: the coast, the mountains, the Central Valley, and the desert. The coast is a strip of land more than 1,300 miles long. It lies between the Pacific Ocean and the Coast Ranges. San Francisco and Los Angeles are both located in the coastal region.

Mountain ranges cover much of California. These include the Klamath Mountains and the Cascade Range in the north. The Sierra Nevada and the Coast Ranges form a ring around the Central Valley. The northern mountains get lots of rain and snow that feed streams and rivers. People in the mountains live in small towns or on ranches or farms.

## The Central Valley and Deserts

The Central Valley is in the center of California. It is more than 400 miles long and about 50 miles wide. Long ago, woods, grasslands, and wetlands covered the Central Valley. People filled in many of the wetlands to make farmland. Because of the Central Valley's rich soil and long growing season, it supplies about half the country's fruits, vegetables, and grains. With little rain in the summer, dams, channels, pumps, and ditches are used to bring water.

California's deserts are east of its mountains. The mountains block moisture from the ocean and receive the rain. The Mojave Desert, California's largest, contains Death Valley. Death Valley has little water, few plants, and very hot summers. Almost no one lives there.

### Before You Read

Find and underline each vocabulary word.

**climate** *noun*, usual weather of a place

**region** *noun*, an area that has similar physical features

**wetland** *noun*, a low area with water on or near the surface

**desert** *noun*, a dry region that gets little rain

### After You Read

REVIEW **What is the difference between weather and climate?** Draw a box around the sentences that explain the difference.

REVIEW **What are the coast and the mountains of California like?** Underline the sentences that give you this information about these two geographic regions.

REVIEW **In what ways are California's Central Valley and deserts similar and different?** How is the climate and geography in these two regions the same? How are they different? Highlight the sentences that answer the review question.

*Practice Book*
3

SECTION **LS**

# Summary: California's Resources

## A Land of Resources

California is rich in natural resources. Air, water, plants, and animals are natural resources. So are salt, coal, and oil. Even sun and wind are natural resources. People depend on natural resources for food, shelter, and clothing.

Each of California's regions has a variety of natural resources. In the desert region, the Colorado River supplies water to Los Angeles and other cities. The desert region also has minerals such as boron, which is used to make glass. Along the coast, workers pump oil and natural gas near Santa Barbara and Long Beach. Farther north, fir and redwood trees are important sources of wood.

In the mountain regions, forests provide wood. Forests also conserve water, helping rainwater sink into the ground. Channels and pipelines later carry this water from the rivers to farms and cities in drier areas. This helps farmers in the Central Valley raise crops during the three growing seasons. The Central Valley is the leading farm region in the United States for fruits, vegetables and nuts.

## Using Resources

People use renewable, nonrenewable, and flow resources. Renewable resources can be replaced if they are used wisely. For example, an orange tree can easily grow more oranges. But if you cut down a 5,000-year-old sequoia tree, it will take 5,000 years to grow back.

Nonrenewable resources cannot be replaced in nature. Earth has a limited amount of these resources, such as gold and oil. Flow resources must be used when and where they are available. Wind, water currents, and sunshine are flow resources. Wind powers windmills to create electricity. Steam from the earth is a flow resource that is made from Earth's natural heat.

People depend on natural resources to live. If we waste them or use them unwisely, our resources could run out. We are finding new ways to conserve our resources. For example, solar energy can sometimes replace oil and gas. People can walk, ride bikes or the bus to conserve fuel. Paper, plastic, and other used materials can be recycled.

### Before You Read

Find and underline each vocabulary word.

**natural resource** *noun,* anything from nature that people use

**renewable resource** *noun,* a natural resource that can be replaced after people use it

**nonrenewable resource** *noun,* a natural resource that exists in limited amounts and cannot easily be replaced

**flow resource** *noun,* a natural resource that must be used when and where it is available

### After You Read

**REVIEW** **Name two California resources and the regions where they are found.** Highlight two sentences that name a resource and where each one is found.

**REVIEW** **Name two renewable resources and two nonrenewable resources.** Circle the resources, and write in the margin "R" for renewable and "N" for nonrenewable.

# Summary: An Ancient Past

## California's First People

Between 10,000 and 30,000 years ago, Earth was very cold, and glaciers covered much of the land. Seas were lower, and a land bridge connected Asia and North America. Many scientists believe that the first humans in North America came from Asia across the land bridge. Others think people from Asia or Europe sailed here.

California's Indians tell oral histories about how human beings were created in California. One story says that gods created human beings while other stories say that animal spirits, such as Coyote and Lizard, made the first humans.

People have lived in California for at least 10,000 years. Back then, California was colder and had more wetlands. Lakes covered areas where there are now deserts. The land was rich in plant and animal life. Camels, giant sloths, mammoths, bison, and mastodons roamed the land. Early people hunted some of these animals for food and clothing. They used spears made of wood and stone.

## Different Communities

The climate in California gradually got warmer. Oceans rose and lakes dried out. Large animals died out. People began settling down in one place. But groups of people were kept apart by the mountains and deserts.

Each group adapted to its environment, making use of the available resources. Over time, people living in different areas developed different ways of life. California's resources supported many communities. A community is a group of people who live together under the same laws.

About 500 years ago, perhaps three million people lived in North America. More than 300,000 people lived in California in small groups. Groups ruled by the same chief formed a nation. About 500 Indian nations lived in California, and over 100 languages were spoken.

These early people built homes along the coast, in river valleys, and in deserts. They trimmed trees to make them grow stronger and burned areas of grassland to enrich the soil. The Tongva first settled in the area that is now Los Angeles. Later, people from Spain and Mexico settled there because of its good resources and warm weather.

# Summary: Coastal Peoples

## Living on the Coast

Five hundred years ago, the California coast was home to many nations of people. There were deserts in the south and forests in the north. Most people in California ate acorns, the nuts from oak trees. Women ground the nuts and rinsed them to remove their bitter taste. They made acorn bread and soup.

All coastal people used the ocean as a source for food. They built boats and hunted seals, whales, and other animals found along the coast. The northern Yurok gathered shellfish. They also caught salmon in nearby rivers. In the south, people hunted tuna, porpoises, and other sea animals.

Northern Indians built homes with boards from cedar or giant redwood trees. In the south, the Chumash used smaller trees, tough grasses, and marsh plants to make cone-shaped homes, that could sometimes hold up to 70 people.

Coastal people made goods from natural resources. They made baskets from grass, reeds, and branches. A large basket could store 1,000 pounds of acorns. Hunting and making baskets were valuable services.

## Trading Resources

Coastal Indians traded with people in other regions to get goods and services they wanted. An economy based on trade grew among communities in California. An economy is the way a group uses its resources to make, buy, and sell goods.

Coastal peoples used barter to exchange goods with people in the valley and deserts. Food, beads, and baskets changed hands. The southern Chumash also traded with people of the Channel Islands. Steatite, a soft stone from the islands, was prized. It could be carved into bowls, pipes, and ornaments. Island people traded steatite and fish for mainland goods, such as acorns.

About 800 years ago, the Chumash created money from a type of rare shell. By about 500 years ago, the Yurok and the Ohlone also used shell money. People who did not have goods to barter could use money to buy stone knives, animal hides, or services, such as the help of a healer.

Find and underline each vocabulary word.

**goods** *noun*, items that can be bought and sold.

**service** *noun*, work people do for others

**trade** *noun*, the exchange of resources, goods, or services

**economy** *noun*, the way a group uses its resources to make, buy, and sell things

**barter** *noun*, the trade of goods and services without money

After You Read

**REVIEW** **What are some ways Coastal Indians used the resources around them?** Put a box around the sentences that describe the use of resources.

**REVIEW** **Why did the people of the Channel Islands trade with people on the mainland?** Highlight the sentences that explain what the people in the Channel Islands traded and what they received in return.

# Summary: Mountain and Valley Peoples

## Central Valley Life

People who settled in the Central Valley and the Sierra Nevada developed different cultures. Like people on the coast, they depended on the resources around them. The Yokut lived in the Valley and in the foothills of the mountains. Also in the foothills were the Miwok and the Maidu. Each culture group included a number of nations that shared a language and set of beliefs.

The Central Valley had many oak trees, so Valley people ate many foods made with acorns. Gathering acorns every year was a common tradition. Some Yokuts built towns near the marshy wetlands of the southern Valley. They wove reeds and grasses to make houses. With reed boats they fished for trout. Yokuts in the northern Valley trapped river salmon with nets.

Mountain people covered their heavier, cone-shaped homes with tree bark. The bark kept out the wind and kept in the heat from fires. They ate acorns and fish and hunted large animals like deer, elk and bear.

## California Indian Religions

Each Indian culture had traditions that guided the way people lived. For example, Miwoks could own oak trees, while the Shasta owned fishing spots on rivers.

Each cultural group had special ceremonies that honored certain events. Shamans, or religious leaders, often led ceremonies. The Maidu held ceremonies to honor the god World Maker. They also had a ceremony to honor the grizzly bear and the coming of spring. Dancing was often part of the ceremony. The Miwok, Maidu, and Yokut all had stories about powerful beings. In one story, Coyote, an animal, created the first people.

Children learned their culture and religion from parents and grandparents. Through ceremonies, songs, legends, and art, they learned their traditions. Some still keep their culture alive by practicing traditions. The Maidu still dance to celebrate spring and the grizzly bear. Some Miwoks make traditional baskets and play traditional Indian games. But today, California Indians are teachers, builders, and government officials.

### Before You Read

Find and underline each vocabulary word.

**culture** *noun*, the way a group of people lives, including such things as its beliefs, language, and food

**tradition** *noun*, a way of life handed down over many years

**ceremony** *noun*, a formal act to honor an event or belief

### After You Read

**REVIEW** In what ways did people use resources in the valleys and mountains? Highlight the sentences that explain how people in each region used resources to give themselves food and shelter.

**REVIEW** For what purposes did California Indians hold ceremonies? Draw a box around the paragraph that answers this question.

*Practice Book*

7

SECTION **LS**

# Summary: Desert Life

## Adapting to the Desert

Much of southern and eastern California is desert. The Cahuilla, Paiute, Mohave, and Kumeyaay were desert people, who, like other California Indians, were hunter-gatherers. They adapted to the desert, moving from place to place to harvest ripe plants or find new sources of water.

The desert Indians gathered over 100 types of roots, seeds, berries, and nuts in the mountains and hills. In the lower desert they fished, and gathered cactus fruit and the pods of mesquite trees.

The Cahuilla people built towns near steady springs or streams. They dug deep wells and carried water from the wells in pottery jars to their crops. They grew melons, squash, beans, and corn. They built summer homes without walls. A roof held up by poles gave them shade. In winter they lived in houses made of brush, wood, and tree bark.

The Mohave people lived near the Colorado River. Each year the river flooded and left behind soft mud. The Mohave planted pumpkins, beans, and corn in this rich soil.

## Government

Desert nations organized themselves and set up governments led by chiefs. Chiefs usually lead family groups, towns, or nations. The job of chief was passed down from father to son among the Cahuilla. In some nations, women could be chiefs. Chiefs were expected to be wise and honest leaders. They did not farm or hunt. The people paid chiefs with food, blankets, and other items. In turn, they were expected to share their wealth with those in need. Cahuilla chiefs decided when the clan would hunt and gather. They settled arguments about property. They met with other chiefs in war councils and decided if their people would fight.

Most California Indians organized themselves into clans, large groups of people who share an ancestor. The Cahuilla had about 12 clans. The Mohave, unlike other groups, saw themselves as one large nation. During wars, Mohave towns fought together and protected themselves.

**Before You Read**

Find and underline each vocabulary word.

**hunter-gatherer** *noun*, a person who lives by hunting animals and gathering plants

**agriculture** *noun*, farming

**government** *noun*, a system of making and carrying out rules and laws

**leadership** *noun*, guidance

**After You Read**

**REVIEW** What did California Indians do to get food in the desert? Highlight the sentences that describe how the desert peoples hunted and gathered food.

**REVIEW** What reasons did people have for working together in desert communities? Underline three sentences that explain how government helped the people.

# Summary: First Europeans in California

## A Search for Riches

According to historians, Spanish explorers were the first travelers from other continents to reach California. Spain sent out explorers to look for spices, gold, and other valuables. One explorer, Christopher Columbus, was looking for a new trade route to Asia in 1492 when he landed in North America. The continent was still unknown to Europeans. Spain's rulers sent conquistadors to North America to search for gold and land. The first Europeans to reach California served under conquistador Hernán Cortés. In 1533, he sent men up the Pacific coast to look for a shortcut to Asia. Instead, they found a peninsula. They thought it was an island and named it California after a popular Spanish book.

## Exploring the Coast

Spain divided California into Baja California, which is now part of Mexico, and Alta California, which became the state of California. In 1542, Juan Rodríguez Cabrillo led an expedition from New Spain (Mexico) up the coast, searching for a route to Asia. He reached the area known today as San Diego. He was the first European to visit Alta California.

Spain had conquered some Pacific islands, named the Philippines after King Philip II. Spanish ships brought spices from the Philippines to New Spain and carried back silver and gold. Queen Elizabeth I of England sent Sir Francis Drake to raid the Spanish ships, since England and Spain were enemies at the time. Drake stopped for a short time in California to repair his ship and claimed the land for England. Spain ignored the claim and sent more ships.

## Barriers To Travel

Explorers sailing to California struggled against wind currents that blew from the northwest and water currents that flowed north to south. Steep cliffs and dangerous rocks along the coast also threatened ships. In 1602, Sebastián Vizcaíno led an expedition from Acapulco up the coast, looking for a safe harbor. He found and named Monterey Bay, but it turned out not to be a calm harbor. After his trip, Spanish explorers didn't return to Alta California for another 150 years, because it was difficult to reach by sea, while deserts and high mountains blocked the way by land.

**Before You Read**

Find and underline each vocabulary word.

**conquistador** *noun*, Spanish word for conqueror

**peninsula** *noun*, land surrounded by water on three sides

**current** *noun*, a strong flow of wind, water, or electricity

**After You Read**

**REVIEW** What were European explorers looking for in North America? Underline the sentences in the first paragraph that tell what they wanted.

**REVIEW** Name two European explorers who visited California and tell what they did. Highlight the sentences that tell what the explorers did.

**REVIEW** Why did the Spanish stop exploring California after Vizcaíno's expedition? Draw a box around the sentences that give the details.

**SECTION** *LS*

# Summary: Colonizing California

## Seeking New Routes

In the 1700s, Europeans were still looking for a route through North America to Asia. In 1728, Vitus Bering, a Danish explorer working for Russia, found a narrow body of water between Asia and North America, now known as the Bering Strait. Bering also sailed to Alaska. Later, Russian fur traders built trading posts along Alaska's coast.

The Spanish feared that Russia would set up a colony in California. For this reason, Jose de Gálvez of New Spain organized an expedition to Alta California so that Spanish settlers could build a colony in California. Gálvez's plan was to go as far as Monterey Bay. Three groups sailed from Baja California in 1768. Two more groups traveled by land. They planned to meet in San Diego, and then continue north together to find Monterey Bay.

Britain also wanted to find an easy water route to Asia. In 1778, James Cook explored the northern Pacific. He did not find a water route, because it did not exist.

## A Major Expedition

Gaspar de Portolá commanded the whole expedition. Portolá was joined by a Roman Catholic priest named Junípero Serra. He wanted to be a missionary in California. The settlers in Portolá's expedition were Spanish, American Indian, and African. The trip was difficult. One ship got lost and took three months to reach San Diego. Another ship sank. About one-third of all the people on the expedition died. The groups reached San Diego by July 1769. Portolá and some of the settlers then went on to Monterey. A priest named Juan Crespi kept a diary of the group's travels. Serra stayed behind to set up a mission in San Diego.

When Portolá's group reached Monterey, they did not recognize it. They went on to become the first Europeans to see San Francisco Bay. Lack of food forced Portolá to return to San Diego. The next year, Portolá took another expedition north and found Monterey Bay. By 1776, Spanish missions stood in San Diego, San Gabriel, Santa Barbara, Monterey, and San Francisco.

**Practice Book**
Copyright © Houghton Mifflin Company. All rights reserved.

### Before You Read

Find and underline each vocabulary word.

**colony** *noun*, land ruled by another country

**settler** *noun*, a person who moves to a new place

**missionary** *noun*, a person who travels to an area to teach a religion

**mission** *noun*, a settlement built to teach a religion to people who live nearby

### After You Read

**REVIEW** Why did Gálvez decide to set up a colony in Alta California? Highlight two sentences that explain Spain's concerns about other countries and Gálvez's idea to solve the problem.

**REVIEW** Why did priests join Portolá's expedition to Alta California? Underline the sentences that explain why priests joined the expedition and what they did.

# Summary: California's Missions

## A Chain of Missions

In the late 1700s, Spain wanted its power and wealth to grow. It also wanted to keep other European countries out of Alta California. Building settlements along the coast would help them meet these goals. Missionaries wanted to convert the Indians to the Roman Catholic faith.

By 1823 there were 21 missions linked by road. The Spanish settlers built forts and towns nearby. The forts protected the missions. The missions were built in places where there was fresh water, rich soil, and resources for building. California Indians did much of the work to build missions. The first missions were built of wood. Later, adobe was used. At first the Indians came by choice. Missionaries offered them gifts. As the mission system grew, the Indians were forced to come. The missions took lands that Indians had used. Then they had no choice but to come to the mission for food. Soldiers also forced them to come.

## Life at a Mission

Indians gave up their way of life to become Roman Catholic. They had to stay on the missions, obey the priests, wear Spanish clothes, and learn Spanish. They worked all day in the fields. Some tried to continue practicing their own traditions. Some missions allowed this, but others did not.

The priests taught the Indians to grow plants from Europe and to raise farm animals. They taught them how to make goods that Europeans used. Sometimes Indians were whipped and chained to force them to convert.

## Resisting the Missions

Missionaries believed they were helping the Indians by making them into farmers. They also needed the food for themselves and the Spanish soldiers. Some Indians resisted their new way of life. They broke tools and equipment or ran away. Some planned revolts. But in the end, California Indians lost their old way of life. They also lost the skills they needed to live outside the mission, and the land once used for hunting had been turned into farms. Without knowing it, the Spanish also brought diseases to California. By 1846, two-thirds of the Indians in California had died.

---

### Before You Read

Find and underline each vocabulary word.

**convert** *verb*, to change a religion or belief

**adobe** *noun*, a brick made of dried clay and straw

**revolt** *noun*, an uprising against a ruler

### After You Read

**REVIEW** Why did the Spanish leaders and missionaries build missions in California? Draw a box around the paragraph that explains the reasons the Spanish people built missions.

**REVIEW** What were some of the jobs California Indians did on missions? Underline two sentences that explain what priests taught the Indians to do.

**REVIEW** What did California Indians do to resist the missions? Highlight three sentences that explain how the Indians rebelled against the Spanish conquerors.

SECTION **LS**

# Summary: Presidios and Settlements

## A Growing Colony

Spanish leaders wanted more people to settle in Alta California. In 1774, Juan Bautista de Anza, a soldier, set off to find a better land route. He crossed the Sonoran desert and arrived at Mission San Gabriel in three months. The next year, he led 240 settlers from Mexico to Monterey. He led others further north to start a settlement at San Francisco.

To protect settlers, Spain built presidios, or forts, along the coast. The presidio was usually near a port, so the colony could be protected. Forts were evenly spaced so soldiers could protect the missions against Indian revolts. A long dirt road connected all the missions and presidios. It was called El Camino Real, "The Royal Highway."

Soldiers did more than guard the missions. They also explored and carried mail along El Camino Real. They captured escaped Indians. Life was difficult for soldiers and their families. There was no school for their children. They often lacked food, money, and even gunpowder. Soldiers sometimes didn't get paid for years.

## Starting Pueblos

In 1771, The King of Spain made Felipe de Neve governor of Alta California. He brought more settlers to California. He wanted them to start pueblos, or towns, and to grow food for the soldiers. He also hoped they would stay and raise families. In 1777, 14 families started the first pueblo, called San Jose. Four years later, in 1781, 11 families started Los Angeles. More than half were African, and the others were Spanish and Indian settlers.

Many of the first settlers were farmers, miners, and traders from Mexico. Soldiers and Indians also lived in pueblos. Settlers received land, tools, and money from Spain. They also got cattle and horses. In return, they built houses and grew food. Many hired Indians to do the work.

Each pueblo had an alcalde, or leader, who had the power of a mayor or judge. The governor chose the first alcaldes. Later, people in the pueblo voted for their leaders. Presidios protected missions and pueblos from attack. In return, missions and pueblos grew food for the soldiers.

### Before You Read

Find and underline each vocabulary word.

**presidio** *noun* (Spanish), fort

**governor** *noun*, person who leads a colony or state

**pueblo** *noun* (Spanish), town or village

**alcalde** *noun* (Spanish), leader of a pueblo

### After You Read

**REVIEW** **Why did the Spaniards build presidios in California?** Highlight the sentence that answers this question.

**REVIEW** **What were the jobs of settlers?** Put a box around the paragraph that explains what the settlers did.

# Summary: Mexico Wins Independence

## Fighting for Freedom

In the 1800s, Alta California was part of the colony of New Spain. The King of Spain governed his colony through a viceroy, or governor. Many people were unhappy with Spanish rule. Unfair laws gave most of the power to the rich people from Spain. People born in Mexico, especially Mexican Indians, had few rights.

In 1810, a priest named Miguel Hidalgo y Costilla gathered an army of 50,000 to fight against Spain. Hidalgo was soon killed. But José María Morelos and Vicente Guerrero led the Mexican War for Independence to victory. By 1821, the Spanish were forced to leave Mexico. Although there were many battles, the war was not fought in Alta California. Mountains and deserts cut off the region.

## The Republic of Mexico

After the war, Alta California became part of the new country called Mexico. The first Mexican government was similar to Spain's. Augustín de Iturbide, the emperor, was soon driven out of office because his rule was too harsh. Instead, a republic was set up, a government in which lawmakers are elected. In 1824, Mexico's leaders wrote a constitution and created a congress elected by voters. They also created the office of president and a system of courts similar to the United States.

## Trade in California

People of Spanish descent living in Alta California were called Californios. Before the war, they could not buy goods from countries other than Spain. During the war, they could not get supplies from Spain, so they began trading with Americans and Russians. The first trading post was set up at Fort Ross. Californios from San Francisco bought imports, such as cloth and tools. They traded wheat, salt, and other food to the Russians at Fort Ross. These were their exports. Californios sold cow hides and tallow, or fat, to Yankees. Hides were used to make leather goods. Tallow was used for candles.

# Summary: Mexico and California

## Change in Alta California

When Mexico gained its independence from Spain, Alta California accepted Mexican rule. They became Mexican citizens. All citizens, whether of Indian or Spanish descent, were to be treated equally under Mexican law. Still, California Indians continued to be treated unfairly.

Mexico appointed Luís Antonio Argüello as the governor of Alta California. Argüello was the first governor born there. He set up a diputación to make laws. But the diputación had little power. Leaders in Mexico had to approve any laws that were made.

## The End of the Missions

Under Spain's rule, the missions had owned most of the land that was best for raising cattle. Many Californios called for the missions to be closed. Some of them hoped to free the Indians living there. Others wanted the land.

Mexico wanted people to use the land for farming and ranching, to make the economy stronger. The Mexican government began a process of secularization. They took the church lands and property and gave them away. The missions lost most of their power and wealth.

Between 1834 and 1846, officials made about 700 land grants. More than eight million acres of land were given away. Half the lands were supposed to be given to California Indians. But the government did not divide the land fairly between the Indians and Californios. Most of the land grants went to rich Californios and new settlers. Some wealthy Californios bought land from the Indians. Others cheated to get the land. California Indians ended up with very little of their own land. Much of the land was turned into large ranchos. Many California Indians stayed to work on the ranchos. Some tried to return to their old ways of life.

Mexico allowed ranchos to trade with people from other countries. Exports of cow hides and tallow made the economy of Alta California stronger.

**Before You Read**

Find and underline each vocabulary word.

**secularization** *noun*, process by which the government takes control of church property
**land grant** *noun*, a piece of land given away by the government
**rancho** *noun* (Spanish), a cattle ranch

**After You Read**

REVIEW What part of California's government changed under Mexican rule? Draw a box around the paragraph that describes a change in the government.

REVIEW What steps did Mexico take to change California's economy? Highlight the sentences that explain how land ownership was changed to strengthen the economy.

# Summary: Ranchos and Pueblos

## The Rise of the Ranchos

Cattle were a major part of the economy in Alta California. Rancheros and rancheras raised cattle for the hides and tallow. People made boots and other leather goods from the hides. Tallow was used to make candles. Traders from the United States and Britain sailed to Alta California for these goods. They paid with clothing, furniture, and other finished goods. Some California families grew very wealthy.

Some wealthy rancheros and rancheras kept thousands of cattle. One ranchero owned most of the Sonoma Valley. Large families, including parents, grandparents, and children often lived together on the ranchos. Many people worked on ranchos, including farmers, weavers, and cooks. Twice a year, vaqueros rounded up the cattle. This was called a rodeo. In the spring, the vaqueros branded the calves. In the fall, cattle were chosen for their hides. After a rodeo, the rancho held a fiesta that might last for days.

## Living in a Pueblo

As ranchos grew, so did pueblos. Hides and tallow were stored in warehouses in pueblos near the coast. When trading ships arrived, finished goods were exchanged for the hides and tallow. Some pueblos became centers of business.

When a ship arrived, people celebrated with music and dancing. Fiestas were as important a part of life in the pueblo as on the rancho. Another common way of life was the willingness of people to share their food and home with strangers.

Government officials, soldiers, skilled workers, and some rancho workers lived in the pueblos. The voters of each pueblo chose an alcalde and a council. The alcalde acted as mayor and judge and resolved arguments. The council gave advice to the alcalde.

In the 1830s, when the Mexican government closed the missions, many California Indians had few choices. They knew how to farm but had no land. Some moved into the pueblos and did heavy labor for little pay. Some stayed on the ranchos and worked as vaqueros, often for no money. They received clothing, food, and a house.

---

**Before You Read**

Find and underline each vocabulary word.

**vaquero** *noun* (Spanish), a cowboy

**rodeo** *noun* (Spanish), a roundup of cattle

**fiesta** *noun* (Spanish), a party or celebration

**After You Read**

REVIEW **What was the source of wealth for rancheros and rancheras?** Highlight the paragraph that explains how rancheros grew wealthy.

REVIEW **What ways of life did the pueblos share with the ranchos?** Draw a box around the paragraph that described customs the rancho and the pueblo had in common.

SECTION **LS**

# Summary: Trails to California

## Explorers Cross the Frontier

Sea traders brought back amazing stories about California to the United States. Pioneers began crossing the western frontier. The first to reach Alta California were hardy mountain men who explored the mountains and deserts.

An early mountain man, Jedediah Strong Smith, was the first American to reach Alta California by land. In 1826, Smith crossed the Mojave Desert to the mission of San Gabriel and then went north to the Central Valley. The next year, he was the first American to cross the Sierra Nevada.

In 1844, John C. Frémont, a United States Army explorer, led a team to the San Joaquin Valley. In 1850, James Beckwourth, a trapper and trader, found the lowest mountain pass through the Sierra Nevada.

## Pioneers Move West

American pioneers came to Alta California in hopes of finding cheap land to farm. They used land routes, crossing prairies, rivers, deserts, and mountains. The pioneers followed the routes of the mountain men. In 1841, John Bidwell, a young teacher, organized a wagon train from Missouri. They reached the San Joaquin Valley in about six months. His route became known as the California Trail.

The Donner party set off in 1846 from Illinois, but none of these pioneers knew how to cross the mountains. When winter came, the party became trapped in snow. Seven people managed to cross the mountains and send back help to the starving group. Stranded for four months, only about half of the group had survived.

## Sutter's Fort

Another famous pioneer was John Augustus Sutter, who arrived in California in 1839. He received a land grant of 50,000 acres from the government and called his land New Helvetia, "New Switzerland," because he was Swiss. He built Sutter's Fort on the land. Sutter's Fort became an arrival point for pioneers, who were welcomed by Sutter. Meanwhile, Mexico was losing control over Alta California, as wealthy ranchers resisted Mexican rule. In 1845, Pío Pico became governor and failed to slow the flood of pioneers.

### Before You Read

Find and underline each vocabulary word.

**frontier** *noun*, a natural area that settlers start moving into

**trapper** *noun*, someone who hunts animals for their fur

**pioneer** *noun*, one of the first to enter or settle a place

### After You Read

**REVIEW** **What parts of Alta California did Americans explore and what did they find?** Draw a box around the two paragraphs that describe the journeys of two trappers and an explorer.

**REVIEW** **What dangers did the early pioneers face?** Highlight two sentences that describe what pioneers had to do to get to Alta California.

**REVIEW** **What was the importance of Sutter's Fort to pioneers?** Underline the sentence that explains the importance of Sutter's Fort.

# Summary: Bear Flag Revolt

## American Interest in California

In the mid-1840s, California had about 7,000 Californios and was part of Mexico. The families of most Californios were from Spain and Mexico. Under the law, only Mexican citizens could own land. By 1845, about 1,000 settlers had arrived from the United States. Some were trappers or merchants. Others ranched or farmed. They did not obey Mexican laws. Pío Pico, the Mexican governor of California, was concerned. Many settlers believed in "Manifest Destiny," the belief that the United States was meant to extend from the Atlantic to the Pacific Ocean. American settlers wanted Mexico to give up California.

James K. Polk, who became President of the United States in 1845, also believed in Manifest Destiny and wanted California to be part of the United States. Ports like San Francisco could expand trade and protect the United States. Polk also worried that Great Britain might take over California. Polk promised to protect settlers who went to California.

## The Bear Flag Republic

In the spring of 1846, a group of American farmers and mountain men called the Bears decided to rebel against Mexico. Ezekiel Merritt was one of the leaders. John C. Frémont, a U.S. Army officer in California, advised Merritt and the Bears on a plan to capture the pueblo of Sonoma.

Sonoma was headquarters for part of the Mexican army in northern California. Mariano Vallejo was in charge. But he also didn't like the way Mexico governed and thought the United States might do better. When Vallejo was surprised by the Bears on June 14, he invited them in and gave them control of Sonoma. The Bears then declared California free, and claimed it was now the Republic of California. They created a flag with a star and a grizzly bear. The event became known as The Bear Flag Revolt. The Republic of California lasted less than a month, as the United States had already declared war on Mexico in a separate incident.

### Before You Read

Find and underline each vocabulary word.

**official** *noun*, someone in charge of a certain area

**headquarters** *noun*, a central place

**military** *noun*, groups armed to protect a country

### After You Read

**REVIEW** **Why did President Polk want the United States to control California?** Highlight the sentences that tell Polk's reasons for wanting California for the United States.

**REVIEW** **What happened at Sonoma during the Bear Flag Revolt?** Underline the sentences that describe the revolt.

*Practice Book*
17

SECTION **LS**

# Summary: The Mexican–American War

## Neighbors at War

The United States and Mexico could not agree on the border between them. The United States claimed that Mexican soldiers crossed over to attack some American soldiers. Some in the United States said it was just an excuse to get land claimed by Mexico. Others feared that the practice of slavery would spread to new land gained by war.

Most of Congress as well as President Polk were for the war. They believed in Manifest Destiny, and Polk wanted California. In May 1846, the United States declared war. It became known as the Mexican–American War.

News of the war took more than a month to reach California. On July 2, Commodore John D. Sloat, a commander of U.S. Navy ships in the Pacific, waited for news. He had orders to take California ports when war broke out. He decided to take action on July 7, and raised the American flag over Monterey. Yerba Buena and San Francisco Bay were captured, and Commodore Robert Stockton took San Diego and Los Angeles.

## California and the War

While the U.S. Navy defended the coast of California, General Stephen Watts Kearney led U.S. Army troops on land. Kearney's troops drove some of the Mexican troops back to Mexico. Californios in the Mexican army were left to fight the Americans alone.

As a U.S. Army officer, John Frémont led the Bears and other troops. In January 1847, Frémont arrived in Santa Barbara. A Californio woman named Bernarda Ruiz convinced Frémont to make peace with Californio leaders. Ruiz also spoke with General Andrés Pico, a Californio leader. He agreed to the Treaty of Cahuenga, which ended the fighting in California.

The war continued outside California, until the United States defeated Mexico. The Treaty of Guadalupe Hidalgo was signed by both sides in February 1848. Mexico was forced to give much of the territory of California, Texas, Arizona, and New Mexico to the United States. California was now part of the United States.

## Before You Read

Find and underline each vocabulary word.

**slavery** *noun*, the practice of buying and selling people and forcing them to work without pay

**armed forces** *noun*, groups organized to protect a country

**treaty** *noun*, a written agreement between countries

**territory** *noun*, land that belongs to a country

## After You Read

**REVIEW** **Why did the United States go to war with Mexico?** Highlight the sentences that explain what the United States wanted.

**REVIEW** **Who took part in ending the fighting in California during the Mexican–American War?** Underline the sentences that tell how fighting ended in California.

# Summary: The Gold Rush

## News of Gold

Around the time California became part of the United States in 1848, John A. Sutter hired carpenter John Marshall to build a sawmill on the American River. Marshall hired Indians to dig a ditch for water to power the mill. On January 24, 1848, they found some tiny, shiny rocks. Marshall took them to Sutter, who tested them. The rocks were gold.

The men tried to keep it a secret, but word got out. Sam Brennan, a San Francisco merchant, wanted to sell shovels. He announced the discovery of gold to people in the streets, and the gold rush began. Many of the first miners were Californios. Nearly half were Indians hired to work for Californios or Americans.

In December 1848, President Polk announced in a speech that there really was more gold in California than people had thought. Suddenly, thousands got "gold fever" and headed west. During 1849, 80,000 people joined the California Gold Rush. They were called forty-niners.

## Three Routes

Forty-niners came from many places, especially the eastern United States. They arrived by three routes. The most popular and cheapest was by land. It took six months by wagon. People had to cross swift rivers and high mountains, facing harsh weather, hunger, and thirst. The second most popular route was by sea. People sailed around the tip of South America and up to California. Boat tickets were more expensive, but sailing was less difficult and dangerous.

A third route combined land and sea travel. People sailed to Central America and crossed the isthmus by riverboat and mule. After reaching the Pacific Ocean, travelers took ships to California. This journey took about three months.

Between 1848 and 1854, about 300,000 people came to California. About 75,000 were immigrants from Chile, China, Great Britain, and other countries. These immigrants brought great diversity, changing the culture of California.

---

### Before You Read

Find and underline each vocabulary word.

**gold rush** *noun*, when many people rush to a place in search of gold

**forty-niner** *noun*, someone who went to California in 1849 to look for gold

**isthmus** *noun*, a narrow strip of land between two larger pieces of land

---

### After You Read

**REVIEW** Why did the forty-niners head to California? Draw a box around the paragraph that explains why people headed west.

**REVIEW** What three routes brought miners from the East Coast to California? Highlight the sentences that tell how miners traveled to California.

*Practice Book*

19

SECTION **LS**

# Summary: Life in the Goldfields

## Mining Gold

Gold is a valuable natural resource because it is rare. The region near Sutter's Mill was one of the few places in the world where people found gold in large amounts. The goldfields of California included the rivers and mountains of the Sierra Nevada.

Gold forms deep in the Earth. When erosion wears away soil, gold nuggets can wash into rivers and streams. Since gold is heavier than sand or gravel, early miners used a technology called panning. They swirled water and sand in a pan and then poured out the sand, leaving the heavier gold on the bottom. Within a few years, miners took most of the gold from the streams and rivers.

To get more gold, miners dug deeper into the earth. They used the technology of hydraulic mining. Jets of water were used to wash away hillsides to uncover gold. Miners also used gunpowder to blast away rock and soil. They cut down trees to build mine shafts. They dug tunnels. The miners hurt forests, flooded farmland, and later poisoned water. The gold rush damaged land and lives.

## Life in Mining Camps

Life in the goldfields was tough. Many miners worked from sunup to sundown. They might find gold, but not enough to make them rich. When work was done, there were few places to buy food. Early miners often lived in tents on their claims. Some claims were just ten feet wide. There were no police to stop quarrels. Fires could also spread quickly.

Immigrant miners and Indians faced discrimination. An unjust law, called the Foreign Miners' Tax of 1850, forced immigrants to pay $20 a month to mine. That was a great deal of money then. Discrimination also forced the Chinese and many others to set up their own separate camps.

Over time, camp life changed. People built cabins and houses. The camps grew into towns with shops, restaurants, and gathering places. Some camps published newspapers. Much of what we know about camp life comes from old newspapers, journals, and letters.

### Before You Read

Find and underline each vocabulary word.

**technology** *noun*, the use of tools and scientific knowledge to get things done

**hydraulic mining** *noun*, the use of hoses with jets of water to uncover gold from hillsides

**discrimination** *noun*, the unfair treatment of people because they are members of a certain group

### After You Read

REVIEW **What were three technologies the early gold miners used?** Highlight sentences that explain the ways in which people mined for gold.

REVIEW **What are some ways people today know about life in mining camps?** Underline the sentences that tell our sources of information.

*Practice Book*

20

# Summary: Business Booms

## Businesses Grow

During the Gold Rush businesses boomed. Between 1849 and 1855, almost 200,000 people came to California. They were nearly all consumers, who needed goods and services.

Miners needed food. People started farms, grocery stores, bakeries, and restaurants. New stores sold food, shovels and tools, blankets, and clothes. Laundries and blacksmith shops sold services that people needed. New businesses could charge high prices because the demand for goods and services was high.

The mining business also grew. In the early days, gold was easy to find along rivers and streams. After the surface gold was gone, miners dug deeper and bought more expensive equipment, such as hoses for hydraulic mining. Some started mining companies and hired many others to dig tunnels. Big businesses helped other businesses, such as banks, grow.

## Gold Rush Entrepreneurs

During the Gold Rush, many entrepreneurs started businesses. Domenico Ghirardelli, for example, was a candy maker from Italy, who found little gold. He opened a general store in Stockton that burned down in 1851. Ghirardelli went back to candy making. His company became known for its chocolates.

Levi Strauss was another entrepreneur whose family came from Europe. They sold cloth and other goods in New York City. In 1853, Strauss opened a branch of the business in San Francisco. Most of his customers sold supplies to miners. About 20 years later, his company created the popular work pants known today as blue jeans.

Luzena Stanley Wilson built a hotel in Nevada City called El Dorado. She charged $25 per week to sleep and eat in her hotel. Lucy Stoddard Wakefield baked 240 pies each week and sold them for $1.00 each. Another woman made $20,000 cooking hot meals for miners. She made more money than many miners.

**Before You Read**

Find and underline each vocabulary word.

**profit** *noun*, the money left over after all the costs of running a business are paid

**consumer** *noun*, someone who buys goods or services from a business

**supply** *noun*, the amount of something businesses will create for a certain price

**entrepreneur** *noun*, a person who takes a risk to start and run a business

**After You Read**

REVIEW What were some types of businesses that sold things to miners? Highlight the sentences that tell what businesses provided.

REVIEW How did some entrepreneurs make money during the Gold Rush? Underline sentences that describe particular businesses.

# Summary: The Thirty-first State

## Reasons for a State

When California became part of the United States in 1848, it did not become a state. The governor was a U.S. Army officer. Most of California's pueblos were still governed by the alcaldes appointed by Mexico's government. After the Gold Rush, newcomers greatly outnumbered Californios. Since many newcomers were from the United States, they wanted the same rights and freedoms they had in their home state. They wanted California to be a state, so they could vote for leaders to represent them in the U.S. Congress. Californios hoped the land would be declared an official territory. The governor agreed only that California needed a better system of government.

## A Constitutional Convention

In 1849, the governor General Riley called for a convention to write a constitution. Americans and Californios voted for delegates to the constitutional convention. The delegates created a state constitution to outline how the people of California would be governed. They decided that only white men would have voting rights. Delegates also agreed to outlaw slavery. The new Constitution began with a "Declaration of Rights" that included the right to happiness and safety. California's Constitution included the rights of married women, not yet found in any other state. The delegates decided California's eastern border should be along the Sierra Nevada and Colorado River.

## Statehood

When the new constitution was ready, the delegates sent a request for statehood to the U.S. Congress. At that time, there were 15 free states and 15 slave states in the United States. People from the southern slave states did not want California to come in and upset the balance. After almost a year, Congress reached the Compromise of 1850. The southern states accepted California as a free state. In return, northern states agreed to a law that made it illegal to help slaves escape to free states. The Compromise changed the lives of many former slaves. California became the 31st state on September 9, 1850.

### Before You Read

Find and underline each vocabulary word.

**convention** *noun*, a meeting that brings people together for a common purpose

**delegate** *noun*, a representative chosen to speak or act for others

**compromise** *noun*, an agreement that gives something to both sides

### After You Read

**REVIEW** **Why did many people in California want to form a state?** Draw a box around the sentences that tell why.

**REVIEW** **What was the purpose of California's Constitution?** Underline the sentence that explains why California needed a constitution.

**REVIEW** **What were two rights included in the California Constitution?** Highlight sentences that list a right given in the constitution.

# Summary: New Towns and Cities

## Building Towns

During the Gold Rush, so many newcomers came to California that some mining camps became towns. Some small towns before the Gold Rush became cities.

In 1848, Yerba Buena was a village with 200 people. The Gold Rush brought ships with thousands of forty-niners, and by 1849, the population grew to about 25,000. Its name was changed to San Francisco. By 1860, San Francisco was a busy port of 60,000 people. Ships brought mining supplies and products from all over the world. These goods were traded for gold and items made in California.

Mudville, on the San Joaquin River, was a mining camp. Charles Weber bought it and decided to turn it into a business center. People paid him to open shops, hotels, and banks. The town was renamed Stockton after a war hero.

John Sutter built a road from his fort to the Sacramento River. Stores opened as ships arrived with gold seekers, and the port grew. More businesses were added to the town, which became known as Sacramento.

## Seeking Success

By the 1850s, the Gold Rush had brought people from all over the world to California. The population was diverse. Some people wanted new opportunities and were willing to work hard.

Mifflin Wistar Gibbs came in search of gold but found work shining shoes. He and another man opened a shoe store in San Francisco. In 1855, Gibbs began publishing California's first African American newspaper. Gibbs later became a lawyer and judge and worked for justice. During the Gold Rush, justice was in short supply.

Many criminals came to California to steal gold, money, and mining claims. New mining towns often did not take the time to set up strong government and fair laws. There were few police. As a result, some people became vigilantes. They took the law into their own hands and often committed crimes, punishing and even killing people without proving they were criminals. They often targeted immigrants, African Americans, and American Indians.

---

### Before You Read

Find and underline each vocabulary word.

**capitol** *noun*, a building for work of government

**justice** *noun*, fair treatment of all people under the law

**vigilante** *noun*, a person who takes the law into his or her own hands

### After You Read

**REVIEW** **Why did San Francisco and Stockton grow during the Gold Rush?** Underline the sentences that explain the growth of these cities.

**REVIEW** **What were some opportunities and problems for people who came to California?** Highlight the sentences that show what types of people came to California and the results.

---

*Practice Book*
23

SECTION LS

# Summary: Land Rights

## Californio Lands

Most Californios raised cattle on large areas of land. Many had owned their lands since the time of Spanish rule. Others had been granted land from the Mexican government. All of them had property rights under the Treaty of Guadalupe-Hidalgo, which ended the Mexican–American War. But many newcomers to California wanted these lands. Some moved onto the land and became squatters. They fought the Californios with guns and knives. To settle these conflicts, the U.S. Congress passed the Land Act of 1851.

The Land Commission was set up to settle conflicts about land ownership. Californios had to prove their ownership of land. Some people had ownership papers that were so old they could not be found or were difficult to understand. The Commission looked at over 800 cases and decided on the side of Californios in more than 600 cases. But many people had paid so much money to lawyers they were forced to sell their land anyway.

## Reservations

Newcomers were also in conflict with the Indians over land. They wanted to start farms or businesses on Indian lands. The U.S. government decided to solve this problem by moving Indians onto reservations. Between 1851 and 1852, some California Indian leaders signed treaties, agreeing to move their people to reservations with resources. The treaties, however, were not accepted by the U.S. Congress. The Indians were forced to move to lands with few resources. Thousands died from disease, starvation and attacks. Between 1848 and 1870, the number of Indians dropped from 150,000 to 50,000.

Some Indians fought for their land. The Modoc of Northern California were attacked by U.S. soldiers in 1872. Under their leader, Kintpuash, they fought for eight months. In the end they lost, and had to give up their land. The U.S. government put them on a reservation far from their home. Many decades later the government finally protected their rights as citizens.

### Before You Read

Find and underline each vocabulary word.

**property right** *noun*, a person's right to own and control land, or property

**squatter** *noun*, person who lives on land without the owner's permission

**commission** *noun*, a group of people that meet to solve a problem

**reservation** *noun*, land set aside for American Indians

### After You Read

REVIEW **What was the job of the Land Commission?** Highlight the sentence that tells the Commission's purpose.

REVIEW **Why did the U.S. government move California Indians to reservations?** Underline the sentences that explain the land disputes between Indians and newcomers and how the government solved them.

# Summary: Linking East and West

## Cut Off in California

In 1850, California was farther away from the nation's capital than any other state. More than 1,000 miles of mostly unsettled land separated California from the nearest states. Communication between California and the rest of the country was slow.

Mail and goods moved as quickly as the transportation that carried it. Railroads did not reach as far as California. The land route by wagon was slow. Ships sailing around the tip of South America took about six months. Goods sent by ship could be sunk or stolen. A Californian who sent a letter to a friend on the East Coast might wait a year for a reply. State leaders wanted to know decisions made by the national government. Shops waited a long time to receive their orders, and some goods never arrived. Business owners paid the costs of losses and delays. Goods in California were more expensive than in other places.

## Better Communication

In 1857, the U.S. government passed the Overland California Mail Act. This law set aside money to create faster mail service to California. The government put John Butterfield in charge of the Overland Mail Company. He used stagecoaches to deliver mail. At the end of each stage, fresh horses and drivers took over. This method cut mail delivery time to California to 25 days.

In 1860 and 1861, swift horses ridden by teenaged boys did the most to speed up mail service. The Pony Express used these boys to carry mail between California and Missouri, changing horses frequently. Sometimes they passed their mailbags to new riders. The riders could reach California in about 10 days.

But in 1844, Samuel F.B. Morse sent the first telegraph message in only a few minutes. The telegraph used electric signals to send messages over wires. Wires quickly went up throughout the eastern United States. By 1861, the Western Union company completed a telegraph line across the country.

---

### Before You Read

Find and underline each vocabulary word.

**communication** *noun*, sharing information with other people

**transportation** *noun*, a way of moving people and goods

**telegraph** *noun*, uses electrical signals to send messages over wires

### After You Read

**REVIEW** Why was mail between California and the rest of the United States so slow? Highlight the sentences that give details about the slowness of the mail service.

**REVIEW** What did stagecoaches, the Pony Express, and the telegraph have in common? Draw a box around sentences that tell how these methods of communication cut down on the amount of time needed for information to cross the country.

---

SECTION **LS**

# Summary: A Railroad to California

## A Transcontinental Railroad

Trains were the fastest form of travel in 1861. But there was no railroad connecting California to the rest of the country. Theodore Judah, an engineer who planned railroads, convinced four California investors to build a transcontinental railroad. The "Big Four," Leland Stanford, Charles Crocker, Collis Huntington, and Mark Hopkins, started the Central Pacific Railroad Company. In 1862, Congress passed the Pacific Railway Act, which set aside money for the railroad. Part of this money was paid to the Central Pacific Company to build track east from California. The Union Pacific Company received the rest of the money to build track west from Nebraska.

## Building the Railroad

In 1863, the Central Pacific Company began to build track east from Sacramento, across the rugged Sierra Nevada. Workers cut passes in hills and built tunnels. They filled in low land and built bridges across deep, wide valleys. Laborers used picks, shovels, axes, and wheelbarrows. Work went slowly. The company needed 4,000 more laborers. In 1865, the company hired Chinese immigrants. Meanwhile, the Union Pacific laid track westward from Omaha, using mostly Irish immigrant workers. After six years, the two lines met near Promontory Point, Utah, and were joined with a golden spike. The new railroad increased trade. Towns were built beside the tracks, and thousands of new settlers came to California. Central Pacific earned millions of dollars from its land in California.

## Completing the Railroad

After 1865, most people building track for the Central Pacific were Chinese immigrants, who became known for their skill. Chinese laborers used gunpowder to blast rock from cliffs. They dug tunnels through the mountains during winters of heavy snow and dangerous snow slides. They built passages under the snow to reach work. Chinese workers earned less than $1 per day and worked 12 to 14 hours per day. In 1867, 2,000 Chinese workers went on strike. They wanted about 35 cents a week more and a 10-hour work day. The strike lasted a week. Nothing was changed.

### Before You Read

Find and underline each vocabulary word.

**transcontinental** *adjective*, describes something that crosses a continent

**engineer** *noun*, a person who designs and builds things

**investor** *noun*, someone who puts money into a business

**strike** *noun*, when workers stop doing their jobs to protest poor conditions at work, or to get higher pay

### After You Read

**REVIEW** **What two companies were hired to build the transcontinental railroad?** Highlight the sentences that name the two companies and tell what they did.

**REVIEW** **What were two main tasks of laborers for the Central Pacific Company?** Draw a box around two sentences that describe what the Central Pacific laborers did.

**REVIEW** **What were two dangers in the work of Chinese immigrants for the Central Pacific?** Underline the sentences that tell the dangerous work the Chinese laborers had to do to lay track.

# Summary: Newcomers in California

## Moving to California

Millions of immigrants came to the United States during the 1800s and 1900s. Many went to California in search of jobs. Between 1848 and 1882, about 300,000 Chinese immigrants arrived, mostly in California. They worked in agriculture, mining, and industry. In the late 1870s, the number of jobs decreased, and many workers in California believed the Chinese were taking their jobs. In 1882, Congress passed the Chinese Exclusion Act. Chinese workers could no longer immigrate. The government turned back about a third of the Chinese immigrants trying to enter the country.

## Farm Workers from Asia

Farmers who had hired the Chinese now hired other Asian workers. By 1909, almost half of all farm workers in California were Japanese. Many became successful farmers, bringing new ways of farming and new crops, such as strawberries. By 1920, nearly 75,000 Japanese lived in California. Some Korean immigrants also arrived around 1900. From 1908 to 1910, Sikhs from India and Pakistan came to work on the railroads and then on farms.

Like the Chinese, the new groups faced discrimination. Korean and Japanese children had to attend separate schools. In 1924, Congress passed the Immigration Act, which limited immigration from all countries. But in 1898, the Philippines became a U.S. territory. Filipinos were now U.S. citizens and could freely move to the United States. In the 1920s, more than 30,000 Filipinos came.

## A New Start

In the early 1900s, war in Mexico drove thousands of Mexicans north. Well-to-do Mexicans started businesses in California. Laborers worked in the booming farm industry. By 1930, nearly one and a half million people from Mexico lived in the United States. Many African Americans from southern states also came to California to work on farms and later in lumber mills. By 1900, nearly 8,000 lived throughout the state, some for a while in their own town. Mexicans and African Americans faced a great deal of discrimination.

### Before You Read

Find and underline each vocabulary word.

**immigration** *noun*, the movement of people from one country to another

**exclusion** *noun*, the practice of keeping people out

### After You Read

**REVIEW** Why did Congress pass the Chinese Exclusion Act? Highlight the sentence that explains why Americans wanted to exclude the Chinese.

**REVIEW** Why were Filipinos allowed to move to the United States when other Asians were not? Underline the sentences that explain how Filipinos got the right to move to the United States.

**REVIEW** Why did Mexican immigrants come to the United States in the early 1900s? Circle the sentence that explains why Mexicans wanted to leave their country.

*Practice Book*
27

SECTION **LS**

# Summary: California Farming

## A Good Place to Farm

California is a good place to farm, with soil in some areas that is deep, rich, and free of rocks. The warm climate is also good for farming. In the 1860s, farmers began to grow wheat and raise cattle on large farms in the Central Valley. Wheat needs little water and could grow in the dry parts of the valley. Wheat farms grew so large that farmers needed better technology to harvest the land. New gang plows were pulled by 100 mules. A combined harvester could cut, thresh, and bag wheat in one sweep. In other parts of the state, people grew new crops such as navel oranges. Soon other farmers followed their lead. In 1875, Luther Burbank, a plant scientist, moved to California and developed new types of fruits, vegetables, and flowers.

## Working the Land

Parts of the Central Valley didn't get enough rain to farm. Other lands near rivers and streams were too wet. Farmers used irrigation to bring water to dry areas. Ditches, pipes, and canals carried the water. Canals were also used to drain water from wetlands. But this changed the environment. In the 1870s, only a few farmers and businesses owned most of the farmland and water in California. Newcomers who couldn't buy land worked as tenant farmers. They received a small part of the harvest in return for growing crops on someone else's land. Landowners also hired migrant workers.

## Railroads and the Market

By 1900, California was growing huge amounts of fruits and vegetables. Demand for fresh produce in other parts of the country was met by building railroads to carry produce to distant markets. Railroads fought with landowners over land, and sometimes farmers were killed while being forced off the land. The new railroads were slow and expensive. Produce often rotted before reaching the East Coast. In 1870, the first refrigerated railroad cars used ice to keep as much as 70 tons of apples, grapes, pears, and plums cold and fresh. As technology improved, farmers could ship more produce across the country at lower costs.

### Before You Read

Find and underline each vocabulary word.

**irrigation** *noun*, the use of ditches, pipes, or canals to bring water to dry land

**migrant worker** *noun*, a person who moves from place to place to find work, mostly on farms

**demand** *noun*, amount of a good or service that people want to buy at different prices

**market** *noun*, a place where goods and services are exchanged

### After You Read

**REVIEW Why did wheat farms need new technology?** Highlight the sentences that tells why farmers needed better technology to harvest wheat.

**REVIEW Why did people become tenant farmers in the late 1800s?** Underline the sentences that explain why newcomers worked for the owners of large farms.

**REVIEW Why did farming grow after the invention of the refrigerated railroad car?** Draw a box around the two sentences that explain how refrigeration helped the farming industry grow.

# Summary: Los Angeles

## History of the City

The Spanish founded Los Angeles in 1781 as a farming community with fewer than 50 people. In its early days, Los Angeles was cut off from the rest of the country by deserts and mountains. It had no natural harbor. The Southern Pacific Railroad linked the city to the transcontinental railroad in 1872. Then in 1885, the Santa Fe Railway built a direct line from the east to Los Angeles. By 1920, southern California had as many people as northern California.

As Los Angeles grew, it needed a port to handle the added ship traffic. The best choice was San Pedro, 20 miles south. To make San Pedro large enough for ships, workers deepened the harbor and built a huge breakwater. A freight railroad then linked the port to Los Angeles. San Pedro became the city's official port. The port grew even more after the Panama Canal opened in 1914. The canal connected the Atlantic and Pacific Oceans and allowed for faster shipping to California from Europe and the eastern coasts of North and South America.

## Water for Los Angeles

Many newcomers to Los Angeles started farms. But the nearby Los Angeles River did not provide enough water. In the early 1900s, Los Angeles received even less rain than usual. The desert city was desperate for water.

William Mulholland, the head engineer of the city's water department, decided to get the water from the Owens River, about 200 miles northeast of the city. He convinced people of the Owens Valley to sell their water rights. Mulholland built a huge aqueduct that moved the water through a network of dams and reservoirs to the city. The water first reached Los Angeles in 1913.

But by the 1920s, ranchers and farmers from Owens Valley didn't have enough water to grow crops or raise animals. The area became a desert. In Los Angeles, the aqueduct provided hydroelectric power as well as water for farming and everyday use. However, because fresh water is limited, conservation is important.

### Before You Read

Find and underline each vocabulary word.

**aqueduct** *noun*, a pipe or channel that moves water across great distances

**reservoir** *noun*, a tank or lake for storing large amounts of water

**hydroelectric power** *noun*, electricity created by using the power of moving water

### After You Read

REVIEW Why did Los Angeles's location make growth difficult in its early years? Draw a box around the sentences that explain why Los Angeles's early growth was slow.

REVIEW Why was Los Angeles desperate for water in the early 1900s? Highlight the sentences that explain why the city needed more water.

*Practice Book*
29

SECTION LS

# Summary: San Francisco

## A Growing City

Many people moved to San Francisco during the Gold Rush. It was the largest seaport near the goldfields. As a result, it quickly became a large city. San Francisco Bay has one of the largest natural harbors in the world. The city became a major trade center in the late 1800s. Mills in San Francisco turned wheat and redwood trees into flour and lumber. These were then shipped to Asia, and silk and furniture were shipped back. In 1869, the transcontinental railroad reached Oakland just across the Bay. People and goods could now travel by railroad to the Bay area and other parts of the country.

Many people came to San Francisco to work in factories and on farms. Others who made fortunes during the Gold Rush built huge houses on Nob Hill. Artists came to sell paintings to these wealthy people and settled in artists' colonies. The first cable car line in the country was built in San Francisco in 1873. Underground gas pipes brought gas and lights to streets and homes.

## The Earthquake

On April 18, 1906, a major earthquake hit San Francisco. Many buildings collapsed immediately. People were trapped in buildings, and some died. The earthquake broke many of the underground gas pipes. As the natural gas escaped into the air, small sparks caught it on fire. In no time the city was ablaze.

For three days, more than fifty fires burned. About 28,000 buildings were destroyed. More than half the population lost their homes. Water pipes were broken and fire fighters could not put out fires. Poorly made buildings were not strong enough to withstand the shaking.

The people of San Francisco worked together to rebuild the city. Rich and poor stood in the same lines for water. Architects and engineers studied buildings that had survived to learn what kind of construction best withstood earthquakes and fire. The earthquake showed people how useful cars could be. During the fire, the few cars in the city were the only transportation that got people to safety.

---

**Before You Read**

Find and underline each vocabulary word.

**artists' colony** *noun*, a community where artists live, work, and learn together

**construction** *noun*, the way in which something is built

**After You Read**

**REVIEW** Why was San Francisco's port important to the city? Highlight the sentence that explains the importance of San Francisco's harbor.

**REVIEW** Why did fires start after the earthquake hit San Francisco? Underline the sentences that explain how the fires started.

*Practice Book*
30

# Summary: Time of Reform

## Cleaning Up State Government

In 1906, San Francisco's mayor was arrested for taking bribes. The mayor and other leaders were paid by water, electric, and railroad companies to pass laws to help those businesses make money.

Some citizens, known as progressives, called for reforms. One reform they worked for was to end the power of the railroad companies. By the early 1900s, four men ran all the railroads in California. The Big Four, as they were called, controlled much of the state's shipping and trade. They used their power dishonestly and controlled the government in many cities.

In 1910, a lawyer, Hiram Johnson, was elected governor of California. He helped pass several laws to improve government. His reforms gave government more control of the railroad companies. Changes to the state constitution strengthened the rights of California voters. They could now create laws directly. Voters also gained the right to remove leaders from office at any time.

## Women Work for Change

Katherine Philips Edson was another progressive who worked for change. She led a fight for "pure milk" in 1909, so that consumers bought only clean milk for their babies.

Edson and other progressives fought for the rights of workers as well. In 1911, progressives convinced lawmakers to cut working hours for women to eight hours per day. In 1912, Governor Johnson hired Edson to study laws affecting women's pay and benefits. She pushed for reforms. In 1913, the state government set a minimum wage. New laws also created better working conditions, and employers had to pay medical bills for work injuries.

In the early 1900s, women's groups were working for suffrage. Women such as Edson and Grace Simons organized groups to write letters, make speeches, and march for reform. In October 1911, California became the sixth state to give women state voting rights. It was in 1920 that all women gained the right to vote in national elections.

### Before You Read

Find and underline each vocabulary word.

**bribe** *noun*, payment made to do something illegal or dishonest

**reform** *noun*, an action that makes something better

**suffrage** *noun*, the right to vote

### After You Read

**REVIEW** **Why did some businesses bribe city leaders?** Highlight the sentences that explain what the businesses wanted.

**REVIEW** **List two changes in working conditions for which progressives fought.** Draw a box around the paragraph that discusses reforms in working conditions.

Name _____ Date _____

# Summary: A Growing Economy

## Effects of World War I

In 1914, World War I broke out. In 1917, the United States joined the war on the side of Britain, France, and other countries. The United States sent thousands of soldiers to Europe to fight. California alone sent 150,000 men.

Many supplies for the war were produced in California. Farm production increased as farmers grew extra fruits and vegetables to ship to soldiers. In the San Joaquin Valley, more cotton was grown to make millions of uniforms. Allan and Malcolm Loughead in Santa Barbara built planes for the war. In 1916 the company was renamed Lockheed Aircraft. After the war, the airplane industry built planes for other uses.

Motion pictures were invented on the East Coast. But in the early 1900s, filmmakers began moving to Hollywood for the warm, sunny climate. During the war, millions went to movie theaters to escape worries of the war. Louis B. Mayer moved to Hollywood and helped form one of the most successful movie studios, Metro-Goldwyn-Mayer.

## The 1920s

By the end of World War I, movie-making was the fifth-largest industry in the country. Movie palaces opened in big cities. In 1927, the first movie with sound was introduced.

The agriculture and airplane industries continued to grow as well after the war. But a new industry became more successful. Near Los Angeles, huge pools of petroleum were found under the ground. By 1924, California produced more oil than any other state. Its oil was shipped all over the world. The port of Los Angeles became the biggest on the West Coast. Demand for oil increased after Henry Ford introduced the cheaper Model T car that more people could afford. By 1929, more than 23 million cars were on American roads, almost two million of them in California.

Tourism grew as people drove across the country to California. The state built bridges, tunnels, and hundreds of miles of roads. With new roads came businesses such as gas stations, restaurants, and motels. Cars allowed people to live farther from work, school, and shopping.

**Before You Read**

Find and underline each vocabulary word.

**industry** *noun*, all the businesses involved in making a product or providing a service

**tourism** *noun*, the business of providing goods and services to people who visit new places for pleasure

**After You Read**

**REVIEW** **Why did farm production increase during World War I?** Circle the sentence that tells the answer.

**REVIEW** **What California industries grew because of increased automobile use?** Draw a box around sentences that identify businesses that grew because of increased automobile use.

# Summary: The Great Depression

## The Depression Years

In the late 1920s, businesses and factories began to close. People lost their jobs. Economic depression spread across the country and the world. This period in the 1930s became known as the Great Depression.

In California, the Great Depression affected many industries. Banks closed. Oil companies lost money. People had little money to spend. In 1932, farms made half as much money as three years earlier. Many farmers lost their land. As banks and businesses closed, unemployment rose. By 1932, more than one-fourth of the state's workforce had no work. Without jobs people lost their homes.

By 1934, the country was also suffering from the worst drought in its history. Farmland in many states was ruined, soil dried up, and terrible dust storms turned the sky black and covered everything in dirt. The region most affected by the drought was called the Dust Bowl. As farms in the Dust Bowl failed, hundreds of thousands of people headed to California hoping for work and a new beginning.

## The New Deal

Life in California was difficult for migrants. Jobs were scarce. The migrants in California were called Okies, because so many were from Oklahoma. John Steinbeck wrote a famous novel about the migrants, *The Grapes of Wrath*. When Franklin D. Roosevelt became president in 1932, he convinced Congress to pass new laws. His plan for recovery, called the New Deal, helped keep banks in business and protect people's savings. The New Deal created programs to put people back to work. The Works Progress Administration (WPA) employed millions of citizens to build bridges, schools, dams, and roads. In California, the WPA paid workers to build hiking trails in national parks. One of the biggest New Deal projects in California was the Central Valley Project. Over several decades, workers built dams and canals to control water for farmers. The Shasta Dam helped turn the Central Valley into a rich farming area. But it destroyed important wetlands, a natural habitat of birds and fish.

**Before You Read**

Find and underline each vocabulary word.

**depression** *noun*, a time when many people can't find work and businesses close

**unemployment** *noun*, not having a job

**drought** *noun*, a long, dry period with little or no rain

**After You Read**

**REVIEW** Why did some people move to California during the Great Depression? Circle the sentence that tells why people moved to California.

**REVIEW** What was the Works Progress Administration? Highlight the sentence that explains what the WPA did.

# Summary: California and World War II

## Wartime California

In the late 1930s, war started in Europe. Soon Great Britain, France, and Russia were fighting against Germany, Japan, and Italy. On December 7, 1941, Japan bombed Pearl Harbor, Hawaii, killing more than 2,000 people. The United States entered the war against Japan, Germany, and Italy.

Although there was no evidence, people worried that Japanese Americans would help Japan. In February 1942, President Roosevelt ordered Japanese Americans into internment camps. Some of the camps were in California. More than 110,000 Japanese Americans left their businesses, homes, and farms to live in drafty crowded buildings in a camp surrounded by barbed wire and armed guards. Some Japanese American men, however, fought in a special army unit and earned more than 18,000 medals.

## War Industries

During World War II, California's large agricultural industry grew to meet wartime needs for food. The state also became a training center for the Army, Navy, and Marines. Soldiers trained in deserts, mountains, and beaches, and learned to fly in the clear skies of California. By the war's end, there were over 140 military bases. The state was also a leading manufacturing center. New factories made goods for the defense industry such as weapons, steel, and airplane parts. Shipyards built over 1,500 ships. More planes were built in California than any other state. Before the war, factories hired mostly white men. In need of workers during wartime, they hired women, African Americans, and Mexican Americans.

## Pitching In

During World War II, civilians, including children, saved everything that could be recycled and used for the war effort. They said, "Use it, wear it out, make it do." As the military used more food, civilians were encouraged to raise their own. By 1943, a third of all vegetables Americans ate were raised in "victory gardens." Certain goods such as butter, sugar, and gas were rationed. But the efforts paid off. The war ended in victory in 1945 for the United States and its side.

### Before You Read

Find and underline each vocabulary word.

**internment camp** *noun*, a place where a person is held captive

**manufacturing** *noun*, using machines to make goods

**defense industry** *noun*, an industry that makes equipment for the military

**civilian** *noun*, a person who is not in the armed forces

### After You Read

REVIEW **Why were Japanese Americans sent to internment camps?** Circle the sentence that tells why the government put Japanese Americans in camps.

REVIEW **What new industries started or grew in California during the war?** Underline sentences that describe what California farming and industry did during the war.

REVIEW **What did civilians do to help the United States during World War II?** Highlight the sentences that tell how civilians pitched into the war effort.

# Summary: Peacetime Industries

## Defense and Space Industries

After the war, the Soviet Union took over several small nations and was making powerful weapons. The United States was worried about a Soviet threat. For this reason, the defense industry continued to grow. Factories in California developed missiles as well as faster and new kinds of airplanes.

Then in 1957, the Soviet Union began the space race by sending the first satellite into space. Each country now wanted to be first to reach the moon. California played a big role in winning the space race. California's aerospace industry researched ways to reach space and developed equipment for the space program. By 1965, half a million Californians were working in the aerospace industry. Satellites were built, and the first space probe to land on the moon was developed and built in California. The United States boosted astronauts to the moon in 1969.

## The Leading Farm State

Agriculture continued to grow after the war. In 1947, California became the leading farm state, with about 300 different types of produce, including almonds, artichokes, figs, and olives. California also grew about one-third of the country's fruit.

In California, large companies owned huge farms with thousands of acres of land. They usually grew only one or two crops, and the owners wanted to increase productivity. Researchers invented machines to help pick crops, such as tomatoes and nuts. Fewer workers were needed. But grape and lettuce growers still needed many farm workers to harvest more fragile crops.

During the war, Congress had made an agreement with Mexico to allow farm owners to use Mexican workers, called braceros. They were given food and shelter but little money. After the war, some soldiers wanted their jobs back. But the farm owners did not want to give up the braceros. By 1957, nearly 200,000 braceros worked on the farms. The bracero program did not end until 1964.

**Before You Read**

Find and underline each vocabulary word.

**aerospace industry** *noun*, designs and makes rockets and spacecraft

**bracero** *noun* (Spanish), a strong-armed person

**space race** *noun*, during the 1950s and 1960s, the competition between the United States and the Soviet Union to be the leader in space exploration

**After You Read**

REVIEW **Why did the defense industry continue to grow in California after World War II?** Circle the sentences that tells which industries grew and why.

REVIEW **In what ways did new machines help California farms?** Underline the sentences that explain how the machines aided farm owners.

# Summary: Building New Communities

## Life in the 1950s

Near the end of World War II, Congress passed the GI Bill to help veterans pay for college and career training. It also gave them low-cost loans to buy houses. Hundreds of thousands of war veterans returned to California, and by 1950, California had the second highest population in the country.

Other people, such as African Americans from Texas and the South, also moved to California. Immigrants from Mexico and other Spanish-speaking countries also arrived. From Asia came Japanese, Koreans, and Filipinos.

Newcomers found work on farms and in the oil, aviation, and movie industries. Some started small businesses. Spanish-speaking immigrants in some cities settled in Spanish neighborhoods called barrios. People could not always live where they wanted because of discrimination.

The population quickly increased. More places to live were needed, and orchards and fields near cities were turned into suburbs. Developers quickly and cheaply built homes for many who had never owned a home before.

## Transportation and Entertainment

The new suburbs had few businesses, so people in suburbs needed a way to get to work in the city. California did not build train tracks but freeways. More people bought cars. Gases and chemicals from cars and factories polluted parts of California. Smog became a problem in Los Angeles with its heavy traffic and warm weather.

In the 1950s, television became the popular new entertainment. People could watch in their homes. By 1960, 87% of U.S. households had television. The popularity of television helped the movie industry, as movie studios made shorter movies for TV and produced television shows. Hollywood and Burbank became centers of the television industry on the West Coast. Walt Disney was one of the first people in the film industry to make cartoons for television. In 1954, *The Wonderful World of Disney* began to air on Sunday evenings. In 1955, Disney opened a theme park in Anaheim. Today, millions visit Disneyland and other theme parks in California each year.

---

### Before You Read

Find and underline each vocabulary word.

**suburb** *noun*, a community built near a city

**barrio** *noun* (Spanish), a neighborhood

**pollution** *noun*, anything that makes air, water, or soil unclean

**smog** *noun*, a mixture of smoke and fog

### After You Read

REVIEW **Why did suburbs develop in the 1950s?**
Circle the sentences that tell why suburbs were built.

REVIEW **What new forms of entertainment became popular in the 1950s?**
Highlight the sentences that describe the types of entertainment that became popular in the 1950s.

# Summary: A Call for Equality

## Civil Rights

African Americans came home from the war, after all they had given their country, to face discrimination. Segregation laws in southern states kept black people in separate schools, separate neighborhoods, even separate parks. Reverend Martin Luther King Jr. fought these laws with nonviolent protest. The federal government passed the Civil Rights Act of 1964 to guarantee the rights of all citizens.

In California, segregation laws didn't exist, but people were still treated unfairly. In 1963, the state passed a law making it illegal to refuse housing to a person based on race. The next year, citizens voted to overrule this law. In 1965, race riots broke out in Watts, a poor and overcrowded African American neighborhood outside Los Angeles.

## United Farm Workers

Farm workers in California also faced unequal treatment. Cesar Chavez and Dolores Huerta, joined by a Filipino group, started the United Farm Workers (UFW). They wanted to gain better pay and working conditions for farm workers. In 1965, the workers went on strike against grape growers in Delano. People throughout California supported them by sending food and money to the strikers. Chavez called for a boycott of grapes, and millions of Americans refused to buy grapes or grape products. Growers started losing money. In 1970, they finally agreed to give the workers higher wages and better working conditions.

## Equal Rights for All

In the 1960s, many groups used nonviolent protest to gain civil rights. Hispanic high school students in East Los Angeles fought for and won reforms, including Mexican American studies as well as more Hispanic teachers and principals. Women used nonviolent protests to gain rights. California universities started women's studies programs. More women were elected to national, state, and local government. American Indians took over Alcatraz Island near San Francisco to make people aware of their poor living conditions on reservations. They also wanted to turn the island into an educational center, but they were forced to leave.

---

**Before You Read**

Find and underline each vocabulary word.

**segregation** *noun*, the practice of keeping different groups of people separate

**civil rights** *noun*, rights that countries guarantee to their citizens

**nonviolent protest** *noun*, a way to protest injustice peacefully, without violence

**boycott** *noun*, a refusal to buy, sell, or use certain goods

---

**After You Read**

REVIEW What did California lawmakers do to try to end housing discrimination? Underline the sentences that explain what the lawmakers did and how the citizens responded.

REVIEW Why did Cesar Chavez want to form a labor union for farm workers? Draw a box around sentences that explain Chavez's reason for forming a union.

REVIEW What rights did California women work for in the 1960s? Highlight the sentences that tell what women won.

SECTION **LS**

# Summary: New Neighbors Arrive

## From Around the World

The growing economy of the United States in the 1960s created a need for more workers. In response, Congress passed the Immigration and Naturalization Act of 1965 to make it easier for people to come to the country. People who already had relatives here could more easily join them, and immigration by skilled and professional workers was encouraged. By 1970, most immigrants to California came from other countries rather than other parts of the United States. Between 1970 and 1980, almost half our immigrants came from Mexico. Farms and businesses needed workers, and California is close to Mexico. Mexican American groups in California were already helping Mexicans.

## Coming from Asia

Asian immigrants could more easily enter the country under the new law. Between 1970 and 1980, about one-third of new immigrants were Asian Indian professionals from India, Pakistan, Sri Lanka, and Bangladesh. People from Korea and China also came in larger numbers. Some came because there were few jobs for them back home. Others came to escape unjust governments.

In the 1960s and early 1970s, the United States fought in the Vietnam War. Violence later spread to Laos and Cambodia, creating refugees from all three countries. Congress passed a law in 1975 to help them come here. California is now home to many from Vietnam, Laos, and Cambodia.

## Life in the United States

California attracts more immigrants than any other state in the country. Immigrants come looking for opportunities and a chance to live in freedom and safety. Many become naturalized citizens. Immigration is important to California because immigrants bring new labor, skills, and ideas to the economy. Second, their fresh ideas influence fashion, films, and music. Third, they build connections between the United States and other countries.

---

### Before You Read

Find and underline each vocabulary word.

**professional** *noun*, a person who has special knowledge and training

**refugee** *noun*, a person who flees from war or danger to find safety someplace else

**naturalized citizen** *noun*, someone who was not born a citizen of a country but becomes one

### After You Read

**REVIEW** **What kinds of immigrants did the 1965 law help?** Highlight the sentences that give you this information.

**REVIEW** **Which three countries were most affected by violence from the Vietnam War?** Underline the sentences that tell which countries were involved in the war.

**REVIEW** **Why is immigration important in California?** Draw a box around the sentences that give you the details.

# Summary: Education in California

## Education for All

California's Constitution discussed public schools. Most citizens wanted schools for everyone. But many communities didn't have enough money to pay for schools. In 1863, John Swett became head of the state's public school. He believed that taxes could pay the costs of building and running public schools.

Today, with more than 6 million students attending public school, California has the largest number of public school students of any state. To make it easier to run the schools, the state's schools are divided into districts. The Los Angeles Unified school district is the largest in California, with 750,000 students. Times have changed since schools were just a single room and students of all grades sat together with one teacher. The only subjects taught in those days were reading, spelling, writing, and arithmetic.

## The University System

California's public schools include colleges and universities. The state has the largest system of state colleges and universities in the United States. The University of California, started in 1868, was the state's first public university. Today the public university system includes many other colleges and universities.

Colleges and universities prepare people for many different types of jobs, such as in state government, businesses, factories, and research labs. Well-educated workers help keep the economy strong by providing the state and businesses with well-qualified individuals. Colleges and universities also do important research that improves the health, safety, and well-being of all citizens.

California residents who cannot afford college can get grant money to help them pay tuition and fees. Students who want to be teachers can also get grants. Students with high grades in high school may be able to get scholarships.

---

**Before You Read**

Find and underline each vocabulary word.

**public** *adjective*, for the people

**tax** *noun*, money people pay to the government

**school district** *noun*, an organization that builds and runs public schools for students living in a certain area

**university** *noun*, made up of different colleges that offer programs in many subjects

**After You Read**

REVIEW **How does California pay for its public schools?** Highlight the sentence that answers this question.

REVIEW **In what ways do California's colleges and universities make the economy strong?** Box the paragraph that explains how schools of higher education help the economy.

*Practice Book*
39

SECTION **LS**

# Summary: Technology and Trade

## Leading the Computer Industry

The first computers were very large and difficult to use. But two men—Steven Jobs and Stephen Wozniak—changed the future of computers in 1977 when they introduced one of the first personal computers, the Apple II. People could use it in their homes. The two men grew up in an area in California that came to be known as Silicon Valley, named after the tiny silicon chips inside computers.

Silicon Valley grew up around Stanford University. Professor Frederick Terman, a professor at Stanford, set up a research park near the University. By the 1960s, nearly all the companies that made computer chips were in Silicon Valley because of cooperation between Stanford and businesses. By 2000, nearly half a million people worked there. It is home to computer companies, software developers, and Internet businesses. Another high-tech area, the Tech Coast, stretches from Santa Barbara to San Diego. It's a center for medical research. High-tech industries around Sacramento are also growing. About one-fifth of all high-tech goods exported to other countries from the United States comes from California.

## Trade Around the World

California's location on the Pacific Ocean makes international trade easier for California companies. Many California companies trade with nations on the Pacific Rim. These are nations with coastlines on the Pacific Ocean. The largest international markets for California's goods and services are Mexico, Japan, and Canada. The state's biggest exports are computers and electronic products.

In 1992, Mexico, Canada, and the United States signed the North American Free Trade Agreement (NAFTA), to make trade among them easier. In 2003, California sold more than $26 billion in goods to NAFTA nations.

In 2002, the state opened a 20-mile-long high-speed railroad track called the Alameda Corridor to link the ports of Los Angeles and Long Beach with train yards in Los Angeles. Goods can now be unloaded and quickly carried by rail to trucks, trains, and planes all over the country.

---

### Before You Read

Find and underline each vocabulary word.

**high-tech** *adjective*, short for high technology; it is technology that is very advanced

**international trade** *noun*, trade between countries

### After You Read

**REVIEW** **What made Silicon Valley grow?** Highlight the sentences that explain the growth.

**REVIEW** **How does its location help California's international trade?** Underline the sentences that explain how the state's location helps trade.

# Summary: California's Art and Culture

## Artists and Trends

California has been home to some of the world's most important filmmakers and artists. George Lucas, a film director and producer born in Modesto, is famous for his use of computers to create special effects. His *Star Wars* films are among the most popular movies ever made.

Another California artist is Isamu Noguchi, a famous sculptor from Los Angeles. He created sculpture gardens and playgrounds in the United States, Japan, Mexico, and Israel.

But art can be found all over California. There are art museums everywhere, such as the Getty Museum in Los Angeles, the de Young Museum in San Francisco, and the Crocker Art Museum in Sacramento.

Many trends start in California. Surfing, skateboarding, windsurfing, and mountain biking are some examples of popular trends. The Beach Boys wrote popular songs about California and surfing. The band's lead songwriter, Brian Wilson, came from Hawthorne.

## Many Celebrations

California holidays honor some important people. Martin Luther King Day, in January, honors the life of the civil rights leader. Cesar Chavez Day, a state holiday, is on March 21. On Cinco de Mayo, May 5, some Californians still celebrate the Mexican victory over the French in 1862. Some Californians celebrate the Chinese New Year with parades, fireworks, and dancing to mark the event. San Francisco's celebration is one of the largest in the world.

Old Spanish Days Fiesta is celebrated in Santa Barbara. Visitors to this event learn about the history and customs of the area's early settlers. Immigrants from Denmark built the town of Solvang almost 100 years ago. Every year the town holds a three-day Danish Days Festival to celebrate its traditions.

Other festivals include the Strawberry Festival in Oxnard and the annual California State Fair, a week-long festival celebrating the state's agriculture.

## Before You Read

Find and underline each vocabulary word.

**trend** *noun*, a style or activity that spreads quickly

**festival** *noun*, a day or period of time set aside for celebration

## After You Read

REVIEW **Name two Californians who have contributed to the arts.** Highlight the sentences that discuss Californians in the arts.

REVIEW **What two state holidays honor United States citizens?** Circle the sentences that name two holidays that honor American citizens.

SECTION *LS*

# Summary: United States Government

## The United States Constitution

The Constitution of the United States is a written document that is the basic law of our country. It describes how the national government, the states, and local government share power. The purpose of the government is to protect the rights of citizens.

The Constitution divided the national government into three branches. Congress, the legislative branch, makes the laws. Congress includes the Senate and House of Representatives. Voters from each state elect two senators. The number of representatives in the House a state has depends on the population. California has 53 representatives, more than any other state.

The President leads the executive branch, which also includes many departments. This branch executes the nation's laws. Judges and courts make up the judicial branch, which decides what the laws mean. The highest court is the Supreme Court, which decides whether laws obey the Constitution.

Each branch has limits on its powers. There is a system of checks and balances that allows each branch to check on the others.

## Rights and Duties

The United States is a democracy. This means that power belongs to the people. Our country is also a republic. This means we elect representatives to make the laws. Rights of citizens are protected by the Constitution. These include the right to vote and freedom of speech, protected under the Bill of Rights.

American citizens also have responsibilities. Citizens must obey the law. Adults pay taxes and serve on juries. Many citizens join the armed forces to protect the nation. If laws are unjust, they should work to change them. Voting is both a right and a duty for citizens over 18. Citizens agree to be governed by the person who wins the most votes, even if they voted for someone else.

**Before You Read**

Find and underline each vocabulary word.

**legislative branch** *noun*, branch of government that makes laws

**executive branch** *noun*, branch of government that executes the laws

**judicial branch** *noun*, branch of government that decides what laws mean

**democracy** *noun*, form of government in which power belongs to the people

**After You Read**

REVIEW **In what way is the power of the government divided?** Highlight the sentences that explain what each branch of government does.

REVIEW **In a democracy, what power belongs to the people?** Underline sentences that describe the power of the people.

# Summary: State and Local Government

## State Government

The state of California has its own constitution. It is like the national constitution in many ways. Both constitutions are based on the consent of the people. They are based on the rule of law, which means that the law applies to everybody, and everyone is equal under the law.

California's government makes laws that only apply to the state, but the laws must follow the guidelines of the U.S. Constitution. The state government provides people with many services and sets rules in many areas, including education, and health and safety. California collects taxes for these services. State leaders also make rules on how local elections will be run, who can have a driver's license, and how many days students go to school.

## The Three Branches

California state government is divided into legislative, executive, and judicial branches. The two houses of the legislature are the Senate and Assembly. They try to make laws to solve problems and meet future challenges. The governor heads the executive branch, which is responsible for carrying out laws. The judicial branch includes the California Supreme Court, which has seven judges. Other courts are also part of the judicial branch.

## Local Government

California has 475 cities. In some small communities voters elect city councils. The council may choose one of its members as mayor, or perhaps hire a city manager to take care of daily business. In large cities, voters elect a mayor.

California has 58 counties, each with its own government. Voters elect five people to serve on each county board of supervisors. Members of this group make decisions about county property. California Indians have local governments of their own on rancherias and reservations.

Local governments provide services such as fire and police departments, trash collection, parks, schools, and libraries. The state is also divided into about 5,000 special districts. These districts were created for special purposes, such as recycling, irrigation, or insect control.

---

### Before You Read

Find and underline each vocabulary word.

**city manager** *noun*, a person who takes care of the daily business of running a city

**county** *noun*, a section of the state that has its own government

**rancheria** *noun* (Spanish), land protected for California Indians

### After You Read

**REVIEW** **What is one similarity between the California and national constitutions?** Draw a box around the paragraph that gives you at least one similarity in the state and national constitutions.

**REVIEW** **What are the three branches of California government?** Underline the sentence that names the three branches.

**REVIEW** **What are some of the services provided by local governments in cities?** Circle the sentence that names some of the services.

---

SECTION  **LS**

# Summary: Californians Today

## Where Californians Live

Over 34 million people live in California. The state has more people than any other state in the nation. California has 24 of the 100 biggest cities in the United States.

Some of the larger cities are part of a metropolitan area that includes several cities and their suburbs. Nearly two-thirds of California's people live in the largest metropolitan areas around San Francisco and Los Angeles. San Francisco's population density is over 16,000 people per square mile.

Cities are centers of business, government, and culture. People move to cities or their suburbs to find work. Some places in California have fewer jobs, and people. A region can be analyzed to see where most of the people are located. This is called population distribution. It's important for leaders to know how population distribution is changing. If a city grows, it needs more services. The age of the population is important. More young people could mean a need for more schools.

## Californians at Work

Californians work in many different industries. The most famous, the entertainment industry employs more than 100,000 people. It is part of the service industry, which provides services, such as banks and hospitals. Almost half of Californians over age 16 work in service industries.

The next biggest industry is trade and transportation. Many people in this industry work in stores. About one in ten people work in manufacturing industries, which make goods such as computers or auto parts. In defense industries, people produce goods for military use. Other industries include mining, agriculture, and construction. The communication industry, which has been growing for decades, produces the technology and products that people use to communicate with each other. Cell phones and e-mails have had a big impact on this industry.

More than 22 million people in California work. They need skills to do different jobs. But most people look for work they enjoy.

# Summary: The Challenge of the Future

## A Great State

California leads the nation in many areas. It has the most people and has the most diverse population in the nation. It has one-fourth of the country's largest cities. California is the leading state in agriculture and industry. Some of the best colleges and universities in the world are in California. Plants and animals that exist nowhere else can be found here. From beautiful beaches, to farmland, to stunning mountain scenery, Californians have a lot to be proud of!

In the 1970s, southern California had a problem with air pollution. One cause was exhaust, or smoke, from car and truck engines. Harmful chemicals from the exhaust mixed with the air. California lawmakers passed new laws to deal with the problem. Using a type of gas that creates less exhaust has made the air cleaner. Other states have followed with their own laws about cleaner gasoline. California leads the country in protecting the air.

## Today's Challenges

California is one of the country's fastest growing states. Its growing population needs food, water, homes, electricity, and transportation. The challenge is to find ways to provide these needs while protecting the environment. One way is by California communities recycling glass, plastic, paper, and other materials to keep them out of landfills. Recycling saves resources and energy. Protecting water resources is one of the state's greatest challenges, as parts of the state do not get enough rain. Dams, canals, and reservoirs must get water to people and farms.

But these engineering projects have changed the environment. Damming wild rivers harms plants and animals in the watershed. If people use too much water, underground water sources dry up. Then water is taken from rivers and lakes, hurting the watershed. New technology helps farmers use less water for irrigation. The state has also started some water recycling programs. By learning from the past and taking action today, Californians prepare for the future.

### Before You Read

Find and underline each vocabulary word.

**recycle** *verb*, to reuse materials, such as glass and plastic, to make new goods

**landfill** *noun*, a site where trash is buried in the ground

**watershed** *noun*, a region that drains into a river system

### After You Read

**REVIEW** In what way did new laws make air cleaner in California? Underline the sentences that explain how the laws helped solve the problem.

**REVIEW** What problems are created by dams, canals, and reservoirs? Highlight the sentences that explain how the environment is hurt by engineering projects.

SECTION **LS**